RETURN
OF THE
AntiChrist
AND THE NEW WORLD ORDER

# RETURN OF THE

## AND THE NEW WORLD ORDER

PATRICK HERON

AMBASSADOR INTERNATIONAL
GREENVILLE, SOUTH CAROLINA & BELFAST, NORTHERN IRELAND
www.ambassador-international.com

# Return of the Antichrist

*And The New World Order*



*www.neph.ie*



Printed in the United States of America

ISBN: 978-1-935507-48-2

Unless otherwise indicated, Scripture quotations are taken from King James Version



Cover Design & Page Layout by David Siglin of A&E Media

Cove Concept by Tomislav Spajic *www.clayman.ie*

AMBASSADOR INTERNATIONAL
Emerald House
427 Wade Hampton Blvd.
Greenville, SC 29609, USA

AMBASSADOR BOOKS
The Mount
2 Woodstock Link
Belfast, BT6 8DD, Northern Ireland, UK

*www.ambassador-international.com*

*The colophon is a trademark of Ambassador*

## Dedication

To all those who are seekers of truth.

# Endorsements

"Patrick, I finished your book last night, and I so hated for it to end. It is so informational and spell binding that I did not want to put it down, but made myself read / study / digest it slowly. What a book, what a book. It is so good, and I don't know how anyone reading it could not be so drawn to the savior, our Jesus Christ. You brought so many things to light, answered so many of my questions, and made the scriptures come alive. You have been so used by the Holy Spirit. So enlightened. I have sent your link to so many of my friends, so that they can be informed."

—Pat Poe, Forth Worth, TX

"I purchased your book awhile ago. I've almost finished it, and it's absolutely spellbinding! I came up off the couch a few times in shock that I'd never noticed things in the Bible that I've read multiple times!".

—Krista Riddle

"Thank God, your book put to bed fears I had regarding end times, I can proudly say I found comfort and will continue to find comfort in The Word of God."

—Mervyn Sayers

"I firmly believe that God has brought you on the scene in this hour, and given you insights into the Truth that most in the Church have not had taught or revealed to them. Many who read this book will be shaken to their core by what is revealed."

—Robert Query

"Patrick, I'm up to chapter 15 of your new book. I find it very fascinating and very thought provoking."

—Paul Webb

"Patrick, Your book is truly excellent - I was gripped straight away."
—Ronan Darcy, Dublin, Ireland

"I purchased your book yesterday and could not stop reading it until I got to chapter 18. Then this morning I finished the book. In reading your book, I broke down and cried as I could just see this city coming down. Thank you for this."
—Ken Smith, Parsons, WV

"Your book is great! It's a great synopsis of the genuine biblical view on the Antichrist, in my view, you are the new AW Pink! Congrats, it is well written."
—Jonathan Sieff, London, United Kingdom

"I am almost done with your new book and I have to agree, it's a great book. You confirmed a lot of things that I have suspected and it is written to be really understandable to the lay-person."
—Heather Lowe

" I have the book Patrick and am enjoying it. Thanks for your God given insight. I have studied, and taught the Bible for 30 years now but have never seen some of the things you have pointed out in prophecy."
—Joyce White

"Words can't express how much I learned from this and it makes so much sense. So scary, way more so than I ever imagined."
—Vicky Cornelius

"Hi, I just finished reading The Return of the Antichrist. I will make this brief. I have recommitted myself to Jesus Christ - This book is an eye-opener. Incidentally, I forwarded it to the pastor And he marveled over it and made copies (spreading the word!!!)."
—Joan M Iozzo

# Table of Contents

# Introduction

It is almost universally agreed by commentators that we are in what is called, the Last Days. Because of this, speculation is mounting as to who the Antichrist might be? Down through history, many have been portrayed as this evil leader who is to come and plunge the world into a bloody Apocalypse. From Caesar to Nero and the early Popes, and more recently Stalin and Hitler and even American Presidents, all have been labelled as he. Indeed, a few Christians are convinced that the present leader of the United States is, without doubt, the dreaded Antichrist. However, all of these speculators and commentators have one thing in common. They are all wrong. For the name of the Antichrist, his present abode, and when he will emerge onto the world-stage, is all hidden in plain sight in the text of the Book of Revelation.

The word 'antichrist' appears only five times in the whole of scripture; in Johns' epistles. The definite article 'the' accompanies it only twice. So the words 'the Antichrist' are only found twice in all of the Bible. He does have other names such as 'son of perdition' and 'the lawless one', but these are merely nominal. The reason there is so much confusion over his identity and activities is because most of the commentators and writers on this topic fail to go to the one source we can trust above all else for answers: Holy Writ. Therefore, can we know for certain who the real Antichrist is, or is this information simply not available to us?

In the Book of Revelation, this man is never referred to as 'the Antichrist'. In this book he is called by one name and one name only; **'the Beast from the Abyss'**. How many times is he described as the Beast from the Abyss in Revelation? No less than thirty three times. That is correct. Thirty three. In fact to give him his full title he is called, **'the Beast who ascends from the Abyss having seven heads and ten horns'**. How often have prophecy teachers and End Times writers called him by this title and explained its meaning? Practically none. But this is about to change.

This book is the first in-depth study of all aspects of the man that John the Revelator terms, the Beast from the Abyss. In this volume I will be documenting, from scripture:

- What his name is
- Where he comes from
- Where he is at this moment
- When he will appear
- What the seven heads are
- What the ten horns represent
- His possible association with the United Nations in prophecy
- His demise and final doom

As new born babes in Christ we are encouraged to take the milk of the Word, that we may grow thereby. This book is meat. Strong meat. You will be taken on an excursion behind the veil of the Apocalypse to glimpse secrets that have been hidden from scholars for centuries. It is because we are in the End Times that these mysteries are now being revealed. This book is dedicated to the Most High God and His Son, Christ Jesus.

*Soli Deo Gloria.*

CHAPTER 1

# Will the Real Antichrist Please Stand Up?

WITH THE NEARNESS OF the advent of the coming Apocalypse, many prophecy scholars and Bible teachers have been keeping an eagle eye out to see if they can spot a likely contender who may just be the dreaded Antichrist.

Hitler, Stalin and Pol Pot are names which have been bandied about in recent history as likely fitting his description. Various Caesars and especially Nero seemed to fit the bill in bygone days along with a few of the Popes. Some say an individual called Lord Maitreya is the unholy being. And even a few are fearful that the present incumbent in the White House, because of his good looks, oratorical skills and mass appeal, is indeed the Antichrist in the flesh.

But what of this Antichrist and how can we be sure that we know exactly who he is when he eventually shows up? Are we given signs as to what to look for in this man and what are the attributes specified to him in scripture that can inform us, without a doubt, that this is indeed the person that is to terrorise the world?

This book will provide all the information available regarding this individual so that a clear picture will emerge and provide us with a full description of him. By doing this, nobody will be left in any doubt as to the attributes of the Antichrist and when he finally arrives on the scene, those armed with this information will know exactly who he is. I will attempt to accomplish this task by researching our primary source for truth, the Bible. Before I begin to delve into this important topic, I need to set the ground rules.

That is, I firmly believe that we should allow the Word to speak for itself. I believe that most of the Bible is plain and simple and easy to understand and can be taken literally for the most part. Even parables have a literal interpretation. And where figures of speech are used, we can identify them and seek their literal meaning. Rather than look to events in the secular world of current affairs and draw conclusions from them, we shall go to the fountain of truth, the Word of God, and gather information about the Antichrist from that hallowed source.

One does not need to be a learned person to understand the Bible. In fact, Jesus told us to beware of the Doctors of the Law and Scribes and other well educated religious people who always like to point out how erudite they are in this field and how many Degrees and Doctorates of Theology they possess. A cursory reading of the Gospels will show that the people who constantly challenged the Messiah and tried to trip him up, who organised his betrayal and kangaroo court, who ordered his torture and eventual murder, were the religious leaders, the politicians and the Theological elites.

What was Peter's occupation? He was a fisherman. And Mark? He took care of sheep. And the rest of the apostles? They were 'ignorant and unlearned' according to the chief priests and Theologians of the day. Basically they were a collection of working class peasants most of whom had little schooling. But I bet they were smart people. Peter was a top fisherman and you wouldn't pull the wool over his eyes too easily. Mark was a great shepherd and probably made a decent living from sheep farming. These men were experts in their own fields. They were street wise and intelligent. Perhaps they were not well versed in Theological matters and were lacking in education as regards to the law. But as that great American satirist Will Rogers said, 'Everybody is ignorant. Just in different subjects'.

So if you are a person who has spent years in Theology studies and have the letters after your name to prove it, then you might be at a disadvantage when it comes to ferreting out the truths of the Bible. Better we all become like children and allow that we might learn something afresh from Holy Writ. In fact, if we believe that the Bible is the inerrant truth of God, then none of us should be afraid to change our Theology on a subject if the plain truth is staring us in the face. Even if this means giving up believing in something which we held as truth for many years.

Listen to what the Word says about itself in Hebrews 4:12 (KJV)

> "For the Word of God is living and powerful and sharper than any two edged sword, piercing even to dividing asunder of soul and spirit, and of the joints and marrow, and is a discerner of the thoughts and intents of the heart."

The truths of the Word are so sharp that it can divide between the bone and the marrow. Marrow begins as soft in the centre and then gets progressively harder until it forms the toughness of the bone proper. So this is a figure exemplifying how sharp the Word of God is insofar as it can divide between the bone and the marrow.

It can also divide between soul and spirit and is so sharp it can pierce even between an individual's thoughts and the intentions of the heart. In 2 Peter 1:20, we are informed that the Word of God interprets itself so that it is not left up to us humans to decide what it says or does not say.

"Knowing this first, that no prophecy of the scripture is of any private interpretation."

The Greek word for private here is *idios* and means 'one's own'. That is, no prophecy of the scripture is of one's own interpretation. Because if it is left up to us, we will invariably mess it up which causes confusion and dissension and then division. This has been the curse of the Christian church for centuries. But if we faithfully go back to the scripture and search diligently, we find that in most cases it will interpret itself, thus removing the guesswork and providing us with the truth we so desire. And you can see what English word derives from the Greek word, *idios*!

So the Word will interpret itself if we allow it. For no prophecy of the scriptures is of any private (one's own) interpretation. And it is very exact. The following is a prime example of just how sharp it is, taken from Luke 4:16-21 (KJV):

"He (Jesus), went into the synagogue on the Sabbath day and stood up for to read.

And there was delivered unto him the book of the prophet Isaiah. And when he had opened the book, he found the place where it was written,

"The Spirit of the Lord is upon me because he hath anointed me to preach the gospel to the poor; He hath sent me to heal the broken hearted, to preach deliverance to the captives, and recovering of sight to the blind, to set at liberty them that are bruised,

To preach the acceptable year of the Lord."

And he closed the book, and he gave it again to the minister, and sat down. The eyes of everyone in the synagogue were fastened on him, and he began by saying to them;

"Today this scripture is fulfilled in your ears."

Now this is amazing insomuch as he had to unravel the scroll, for they didn't have books like we have today. They also didn't have chapters, paragraphs or numbered verses. Isaiah was one long continuous document. He unrolled the scroll and found the quote which he was looking for and began reading. But he stopped reading in the middle of the sentence. For if you go to Isaiah 61 verse 2, it says;

> "To proclaim the acceptable year of the Lord, AND THE DAY OF VENGEANCE OF OUR GOD."

Jesus stopped reading half way through the sentence and sat down and said, '**Today this scripture is fulfilled in your ears**'. The latter half of that sentence is still future. For the "Day of Vengeance" is speaking of the Day of the Lord which pertains to the coming Apocalypse and prophecies still unfulfilled. If he had read that next phrase, then he would have been wrongly dividing the Word of truth and your whole Bible would fall apart. But he didn't. He stopped half way through. There was only a comma separating the rightly divided truth of the Word, from error.

That's how sharp the Bible is. It is with this foundation in mind that we approach the task of trying to extract a description from scripture of the coming Antichrist and what his role will be on this earth. If we do not apply due reverence to the task of allowing the scripture to speak for itself, then we do God a disservice. If we allow our own prejudices and misconceptions to guide us, rather than strictly adhering to the revealed Word of truth, then we will fall short of the mark. For we are admonished to be as workmen who study to show ourselves to be approved, rightly dividing the Word of truth. (2 Tim 2:15).

The Epistle of 2 Thessalonians 2 is where I would like to go to begin our quest, for it has some revealing facts to show us concerning whom Paul calls the 'man of sin'. The person who has come to be known as the Antichrist has several names, three of which are given in this passage. He is called the 'man of sin', the 'son of perdition' and 'that wicked', which in Greek means, 'the lawless one'. Where 'the Day of the Lord', which is the Apocalypse, is mentioned, it says;

> "Let no man deceive you by any means: for that day shall not come except there come a falling away first, and that man of sin be revealed, the son of perdition.
>
> Who opposes and exalts himself above all that is called God, or that is worshipped; so that he as God sits in the temple of God, showing himself that he is God.
>
> ...And then shall that wicked (the lawless one) be revealed, whom the Lord shall consume with the spirit of his mouth, and shall destroy with the brightness of his coming.
>
> Even him whose coming is after the working of Satan, with all power and signs and lying wonders.
>
> ...And for this cause God shall send them strong delusion, that they should believe a lie."

The man of sin is also called here, the son of perdition and the lawless one. This is speaking of the infamous person known as the Antichrist. But 'anti' in Greek does not have to mean 'against'. It can also mean 'in the stead of'. It will become clear as we advance this study that the correct description pertaining to this individual is that when he comes, he will be coming 'in the stead of', Christ.

That is, when he shows up, he is going to convince a perplexed world that he is the true Messiah. More on this later. But for now, what can we learn from this passage in Thessalonians? Well the first thing we must glean and get clear in our mind is that we are told that this person is a man. But he is a man that possesses great powers. For it says in 2 Thessalonians 2:9, (NIV);

> "The coming of the lawless one will be in accordance with the work of Satan displayed in all kinds of counterfeit miracles, signs and wonders."

In the Book of Acts we are told that 'signs, miracles and wonders' followed those who believed in the resurrected Jesus Christ. So what will distinguish this man when he comes will be that he can perform signs, miracles and wonders, albeit they will be counterfeit. So the first hint we are given which will distinguish and identify this coming man is that he will be endued with great supernatural power and ability whereby he will be able to deceive the people of the world via signs, miracles and wonders.

So we can now eliminate Hitler, Stalin, Pol Pot, Nero and any other historical figure, as none of these produced any signs, miracles and wonders. We can also omit Tony Blair, George Bush, Barack Obama and any recent leader of the European Union. Neither is there presently a wealthy Arab prince living in the Near East who is Oxford educated and speaks nine languages, who may be the Antichrist in waiting. For none of these have produced any supernatural signs, wonders and miracles whereby they have deceived the peoples of the world.

Having disqualified all the past and present political contenders as possible culprits to be the Antichrist, we continue to search the scriptures for other clues as to his unique personality so that he may be easily identified when he is eventually revealed in the very near future.

Note: Because this material is new to most people and because it is dealing with quite deep and serious spiritual matters, it is necessary to have some repetition of topics so that the information might be digested and understood more easily. Those Christians who are more advanced in the study of prophecy might beg this indulgence as those readers not so familiar may find the information a little harder to assimilate.

# CHAPTER 2
# The Delusion and The Lie

WE LEARNED IN THE first chapter that what would distinguish this Antichrist who is to come is that he is so powerful he can perform signs, miracles and wonders. But these will be counterfeit signs, miracles and wonders. Another main differentiating feature of the man is that he is a deceiver.

Matthew 24 is the seminal chapter in the Bible when speaking of the signs of the coming Apocalypse, which it terms 'the Great Tribulation'. There are many different names given to this coming period of time and I shall now provide a list of some of them. For it is during this Great Tribulation that the coming son of perdition will manifest himself before the world and perform his nefarious activities. Most scholars agree that the length of the Great Tribulation is seven years. But some argue that it is three and a half years. Nevertheless, here are some of the names given in scripture to this coming era.

The Day of Vengeance of our God
The Day of Wrath
The Day of Tribulation
The Lord's Day
The Wrath of the Lord Almighty

The Day of His burning anger
The Great and Terrible Day of the Lord
The Latter Day
The Day of Christ
Christ's Day
The Great Tribulation
That Day
The Cruel Day with Wrath and fierce anger
The Day of Jacob's Trouble

This is not an exhaustive list and there are probably more names provided all pertaining to this coming time. This last name, the Day of Jacob's trouble, marks this future period of wrath as being associated with the Jewish people. But more on that later. Some people say there is a difference between the Tribulation and the Great Tribulation. But I do not see a distinction for all these various names are given and all pertain to the same time-period as described in the Book of Revelation. The Book of Daniel also provides prophecies which are parallel to those written in Revelation. It speaks of the coming wrath but does not make a division in its length.

A man called Gabriel appeared to Daniel and provided him with the visions concerning the End Times. In Daniel 8:19 (NIV) he said:

> "I am going to tell you what will happen later in THE TIME OF WRATH, because the vision concerns the appointed TIME OF THE END."

In Daniel 11:36 (NIV) we have mention again of this time of the end. Speaking regarding the coming Antichrist, who it calls here a king, it says:

> "The king will do as he pleases. He will exalt and magnify himself above every god and will say unheard-of things against the God of gods. He will be

> successful until the TIME OF WRATH is completed, for what has been determined must take place."

There is no distinction here between the Tribulation and the Great Tribulation. For the whole period is called the TIME OF WRATH. This together with the many other names given in scripture which refer to the events in the Apocalypse serve to show that they are all relating to the same period known as 'the Tribulation' or 'the Great Tribulation'.

And in Matthew 24, verse 5, 23 and 24, when asked what these signs would be, the Messiah put this at the top of his list:

> "Take heed that no man deceive you. For many shall come in my name saying, I am Christ; and shall deceive many.
>
> Then if any man say unto you, Lo here is Christ, or there, believe it not.
>
> For there shall arise false Christ's, and false prophets, and shall show great signs and wonders; insomuch that, if it were possible, they shall deceive the very elect." (KJV)

One of the main signs of the birth pangs of the End Times is the rise of false prophets and false messiahs. You can see this all around us today with the emergence of various latter day religious sects ranging from New Age paganism to Wicca and the occult. And from sect leaders Jim Jones and David Koresh to bizarre suicide cults. Other denominations and their leaders who have "fallen away" could fit into this group also. That is, there are hundreds of millions of people who are members of so-called Christian religions whose teachings bear little resemblance to those of Christ. Having been raised as an Irish Catholic myself, I can speak from experience. For despite my strict Catholic up-bringing, I knew little of true Christianity and the Word of God until age 24 when I had an epiphany while reading the Bible.

Living in Ireland, I know many Catholics who tell me of their personal salvation, but the vast majority of the one billion Catholics around the world are steeped in the doctrines and traditions of the Church of Rome and have little knowledge of the truths of the Word of God. They are Christian in name only but this is but a nominal Christianity. I call these group of Churches, 'Christendom'. Referring to the leaders of such churches the Lord said, **'they are blind leaders of the blind. And if the blind lead the blind, both shall fall into the ditch'**.

So the first sign we are to beware of while approaching the End Times are, false prophets and false religious leaders. By their fruits ye shall know them.

But even though the spectre of the coming Apocalypse will be marked by the rise of many self professed false Christ's and false messiahs, the one that will rise above the rest by his supernatural signs, miracles and wonders is he who will state;

> "I am Christ:" and shall deceive many. Matt 24:5 (KJV)

So this man who is to come will literally be 'in the stead of Christ'. This is why Jesus warned us that many shall come, **"in my name..."** He is coming using the name of Jesus and not some other name. He is going to deceive almost the whole world into believing that he is the true Messiah. So amazing are the feats of this man when he makes his appearance on the world stage that, written in the Book of Revelation it says;

> "...The inhabitants of the earth whose names have not been written in the book of life from the creation of the world will be astonished when they see the beast, because he once was, now is not, and yet will come." Rev 17:8 (NIV)

Those of you who are well-read in spiritual matters know that the Devil always counterfeits and imitates what the true God does. Thus the serpent that beguiled Eve appeared as an 'angel of light'. And his ministers masquerade as ministers of the truth. (2 Cor 11:3,14,15 NIV).We are informed in Revelation that this man who will be king, receives a deadly head wound and is killed. But by the power of the Dragon (Satan), he is raised from the dead. This passage is in Revelation 13 and is another major clue in identifying who the Antichrist is. Speaking of one of the 'heads' of the Beast, it says:

> "And I saw one of his heads as it were wounded to death; and his deadly wound was healed: and all the world wondered after the beast." Rev 13:3 (KJV)

This is a counterfeit resurrection and will cause all those whose names are not written in the Book of Life, to worship him. Just as the true Messiah was killed and raised from death by the power of God some 2,000 years ago, so too this coming counterfeit Jesus shall also receive an injury which will mortally wound him. But he shall be raised from death by the power of the Dragon, who is Satan.

One can presume also that like Jesus, he may perform healings and provide food for the hungry. Perhaps he will also change water into wine so that everybody can party and have a good time. For we are foretold also in Matthew 24 that in those days they will be eating and drinking, marrying and giving in marriage, just as they did in the days of Noah. So I reckon it's going to be sex, drugs and rock and roll. All provided for by this benevolent saviour and philanthropist, the true (sic) Christ.

If you want to make counterfeit $20 bills, the closer you can get the dud note to resemble the real thing, the easier it is going to be to fool people. One would need to be a banker or an expert in the field to spot the difference between the genuine and the counterfeit. And so shall it be in this future time. The vast majority of the inhabitants of the earth will have no knowledge of the Bible or of matters spiritual. They are merely what Paul called, 'the natural man'. People of body and soul but no spirit. Therefore not being experts in the field, they are deceived into believing that this man who performs these signs and wonders, is genuine. The true Messiah.

Paul wrote of this coming son of perdition, and informs us that, by deception and sleight of hand, this man will convince almost everyone in the world that he is indeed, the true Christ. So if you see the majority of the inhabitants of earth being deluded by the fine oratorical skills and magical powers of a world leader, then you have another hint as to the true nature of this charlatan.

> "And for this cause God shall send them strong delusion that they should believe a lie." 2 Thessalonians 2:11 (KJV)
> In the NIV it says, "...so that they will believe THE lie."

Many commentators give a range of opinions as to what this lie is that causes such a worldwide delusion. I have even heard sincere Christians say that those believers who think the Church of the Body is to be taken out of this earth in a rapture before the Tribulation have swallowed this lie and are deluded.

But from the context of what we have been debating thus far, it would seem to me that the lie that will be perpetrated and believed by the whole world, is that this man, who will arise in the future, will be the true Messiah, Christ the saviour. It is also prophesied in Revelation that his fake resurrection will be witnessed all over the globe on TV. For we are told;

> 'All the world wondered after the beast...And they worshipped the beast and said; 'Who is like unto the beast and who is able to make war with him?' Rev 13:3 (KJV)

Just as the whole world can now watch political or sporting events, such as the Olympics, happening in real time, so too when this future world leader is killed, the nations of the earth will view his resurrection via live satellite TV links, and will thus wonder after the Beast. One cannot be certain that the lie or delusion which will be believed by the world is that this coming Antichrist is the true messiah. But it would appear logical at this time to assume that this will be the case. And when the citizens of earth witness the resurrection of this man from the dead, then his authority and leadership will be assured.

You have heard of the Four Horsemen of the Apocalypse. The sleeves of many rock albums displayed these dread beings back in the 1960's. The first horse described going forth is a white one, followed by a red horse, then a black one and finally a pale horse whose name is Death. Let us examine the first rider.

> "And I saw and lo, a white horse, and he that was sitting upon it, having a bow, and there was given unto him a crown and he went forth conquering and in order that he might conquer." Rev 6:2 (KJV)

The first sign given by the Messiah in Matt 24 was to watch out for the rise of the one proclaiming; **"I am Christ".** Therefore this rider on the white horse has to be the deceiver that Jesus prophesied about, the False Christ. As stated already, the Devil, who is a master counterfeiter, always apes or copies what the true God does. So in this rider on the white horse we have an imitation of the true Messiah who is to return in glory as King of kings and Lord of lords at the end of the Apocalypse when he shall appear on a white horse from heaven to put an end to this whole terrible episode.

> " And I saw heaven opened, and behold, a white horse; and He that sat upon him was called Faithful and True, and in righteousness He doth judge and make war." Rev 19:11 (KJV)

So the Antichrist, when he goes out on a white horse, has a bow but no arrow. Having no arrow conveys that he is a bringer of peace on the earth. But as the world shall learn, this political leader shall talk of peace, but wage war. In the vision of this rider, John describes the horseman as having been given a crown. This crown signifies authority and later we shall see from whence he derives this authority.

As global peacemaker this man will do something that has eluded Presidents and politicians and world leaders for years. He will resolve the situation in the Middle East and establish a peace deal between the Jews and their Arab neighbours. Prophecy experts extract this fact from Daniel 9:27 which, speaking of this coming leader says;

> "He will confirm a covenant with many for one week." (That is, one seven year period).

Somehow this man will be acceptable to both the Jewish people and the Muslim community and perform this political feat that seems impossible to us today. Thus we now have yet another hint as to the identity of the coming man of sin. He will bring peace to the Middle East. How does he achieve this? Perhaps with a little help from another man who will become prominent around the same time. This man is called in Revelation, the False Prophet, and is also referred to as a beast who rises up from the earth;

> "Then I saw another beast coming out of the earth. He had two horns like a lamb, but he spoke like a dragon." Rev 13:11 (NIV)

Being called a 'false prophet' suggests that this man operates in the arena of the religious. And because of the global machinations of the Antichrist, we know that he operates within the political as well as the religious realm. So how is it these two are acceptable to both the Jews and Arabs and are able to broker a peace deal between them?

It is well known that the Muslims are awaiting the advent of their own Messiah, called the Imam or Mahdi. And the Jewish faith are still watching for the coming of their saviour, the Messiah, (for they believe Jesus was an impostor). Perhaps it is these two who hold the key to understanding the role of the Antichrist and the False Prophet who are to come and pour oil and salve on this troubled area.

CHAPTER 3

# Imam al-Mahdi and the False Prophet

When the Beast from the Abyss inevitably appears at the start of the Apocalypse, he will have another man join him as a powerful religious ally. This man is called the False Prophet. Together they will broker a peace deal between the Jews and the Arab nations that surround them.

At present, the Muslim people are awaiting the emergence of their own prophet who is called the 12th Imam or Imam al-Mahdi. Islamic tradition and holy writings inform us that several hundred years ago the Mahdi, as a boy of about 12, went into hiding and disappeared into a deep well. But soon, they believe, he will emerge from this well to lead Islam in a series of military victories over of her enemies.

The Jewish people are also awaiting the coming of their promised Messiah. For they do not believe Jesus Christ was the true Messiah. So we have two powerful communities both waiting for a charismatic leader to arise and lead them to both victory and peace.

And in the Book of Revelation it is prophesied that two powerful men, the Antichrist and the False Prophet, will go forth as peace makers and broker a deal between these two ancient warring factions. This is the key to world peace. For, without peace in the Middle East between these two age old enemies, there can be no world peace.

Interestingly, the origin of the enmity between these two tribes dates back to the time of Abraham circa 1900BC. Abraham had been married to Sarah, but she was barren and unable to provide him with an heir. She urged Abraham to lie with Hagar her Egyptian handmaid, that she might provide him with a son. Abraham married Hagar and she became pregnant. When Sarah saw this she despised her handmaid who would then run away. But an angel appeared to Hagar and told her to return and submit herself to her mistress. Then the angel prophesied regarding the soon to be born child:

> "You are now with child and you will have a son.
> You shall name him Ishmael...
> He will be a wild donkey of a man; his hand will be against everyone and everyone's hand against him, and he will live in hostility towards all his brothers."
> Gen 16:11,12 (NIV)

Ishmael was the father of the Arab princes and thus the forefather of all of the tribes of the Arab nations of today. Is it not a sad reality that this angelic prophesy has been realised over the past 3,000 years and is evident almost daily in events unfolding all around the world? For many of the bombings and killings and atrocities we see today in Iraq and Pakistan and Afghanistan and elsewhere are perpetrated by Muslims against their Arab brothers. To date, a conservative estimate of the amount of men, women and children killed as a result of the war in Iraq, stands at circa 600,000 people. The regrettable fact is that most of these people were killed by members of their own tribe; **'...and he will live in hostility towards all his brothers'**.

But in the coming time of wrath, there is to be a peace treaty brokered between these old enemies. The prophecy states that the Antichrist, the rider on the white horse, will go forth to bring peace to the world. At the same time the False Prophet, who is described as a beast who shall arise from the earth, will be a religious leader and will play a part in conjunction with the Antichrist in the unfolding happenings in those days.

Could it be that this man, who is coming in the stead of Christ, and who will declare, 'I am Christ', will be acceptable to the Jews as the real Messiah? And by the same token, the False Prophet, who is to rise from the earth, could it be that he will promote himself as the long awaited Mahdi, and will deceive the Muslim faithful into believing that it is he?

The parallels are intriguing. For Islam believe that the Mahdi hid himself down a well in the ground and will emerge from this hiding place one day. And the False Prophet is also to arise from the ground hence : 'And I saw another beast coming up out of the earth; and he had two horns like a lamb, but he spoke like a dragon'. Rev 13:11 (NIV)

All the more so when you realise that the President of Iran, for instance, regularly speaks of the coming nearness of the Mahdi and even predicted that he might emerge last March! And the situation between Israel and surrounding Arab nations is looking more perilous with each passing day.

You might wonder how it is that the writings of Islam, such as the Koran, have prophetic writings at all as we Christians in the West do not believe that they are inspired by the one true God. Indeed you might further contemplate how it is that these prophecies of Islam are so near to the prophecies contained in the Book of Revelation in regard to the coming of these two future powerful leaders. But when you research how it was that Mohammad received his revelations, it becomes clear who it was that provided the dictation for Islamic holy writings.

For we are told that there appeared to Mohammad a bright angel dressed in white and declared to him that he was to be a prophet to the Arab people and that he was to faithfully record all the words of this messenger 'from God'. When we hear this immediately light bulbs go on in our heads and we remember that it was the serpent that beguiled Eve through his subtlety, and no marvel;

> "...for Satan himself is transformed into an angel of light." 2 Cor 11:3,14 (KJV)

Now, the devil knows the scriptures better than you and I. Remember, he was able to quote verbatim from Psalm 91 when he was endeavouring to tempt Jesus to throw himself off the pinnacle of the Temple in Jerusalem. He plucked out a verse and quoted 'It is written'. Of course he was quoting out of context but that is another day's work. The point is, how many Christians would be able to quote directly from any one of the Psalms at the drop of a hat? There are 40 books in the Old Testament and Satan had the appropriate verse on the tip of his tongue with which to tempt the Messiah. How often have we seen scriptures taken out of context by people in order to make a false assertion? It is also interesting to ponder how Satan transported Jesus to the pinnacle of the Temple and then showed him **'all the glories of the world'**, in the blink of an eye? He must have been able to levitate the Messiah to this high vantage point and then, by revelation, show him all the magnificence of the wonders of the world in a moment of time.

Returning to the main point, the devil knows the Book of Revelation back-ways and upside down and must hate this book above all others. And why wouldn't he? After all, it deals with his demise and doom and eternal damnation. So he would need to know it thoroughly in order to try to subvert it in any way he could so as to avert his own final outcome. Thus, as master counterfeiter and as an angel of light, his prophecies will closely mirror the truth of the scriptures and at the same time fit his own plans to deceive the world and cause the complete destruction of man. Therefore it is no wonder to us that other prophecies from non Christian sources would reflect many of the truths of the Word of God, for they were obviously devised by Satan to deceive and delivered by either himself or his representatives who, **"masquerade as ministers of righteousness"**. 2 Cor 11:15 (NIV). There is no surprise, therefore, that Islamic holy writings contain prophesies that are similar to those of the true Word of God.

Incidentally, the Antichrist is often called the, 'son of perdition' which means, 'son of destruction'. The names given to him in Revelation 9 are in Hebrew, Abaddon and in Greek, Apollyon and we are told these mean 'destruction' or 'the destroyer'. Later we are told that this man **'goes to his destruction'**. At first glance this sounds like he himself is going to be destroyed. Not so. It means that he goes out to cause destruction and destroy the world. This is why his name means 'the Destroyer'. He almost succeeds in his task for by the end of the Apocalypse, circa two-thirds of the population of the world are dead. By today's figures this would mean about four billion people are to die in the coming Apocalypse. No wonder Jesus called it the 'Great Tribulation'.

So two men will arise on the world's political stage and will be acceptable to both the Muslim and Jewish peoples. But what of the rest of the earth's populace? Well, if this coming Messiah will be welcomed by God's chosen people, the Jews, it is not a large step to see that he will also be welcomed and adored by the rest of 'Christendom'. Who am I referring to? Well, take me as being raised a Catholic in Ireland. We are considered a Christian country. But it is but a nominal Christianity. For Catholics in this country know very little of Christ or of his teachings. Neither do Catholics in Ireland, or anywhere else for that matter, read and study the scriptures.

Neither do Irish people know of his saving grace, the second coming or who he really is. Proclaiming that Catholics in this country as being true Christians is like me saying I am a motor mechanic, but I don't know how to change the oil in your car! In short, I knew little of Jesus or the Word or the truths of scripture until I had an epiphany as a 24 year old. The same is true, by and large, of all the one billion or so Catholics all over the world. We know a lot about the traditions of the Church and the various rites and rituals that it teaches, but know nothing of the real message of the Lord. It was ever thus. Jesus described the religious leaders of the day as the blind leading the blind. The same is true now of Catholic leaders. And if the blind lead the blind, both shall fall into the ditch.

Sadly the same could be said for many main-line Christian churches. They teach the traditions of men and ignore the precepts of God. They are Christian in mere name but not in word or practice. So when the imitation Messiah arrives claiming to be Christ, and exhibiting signs, miracles and wonders, the majority of Christendom will accept him and swallow his deception wholesale.

The coming Antichrist will be a great orator. Listen to what Daniel 7:8 (NIV) says of him, referred to here as 'a little horn'.

> "While I was thinking about the horns, there before me was another horn, a little one, which came up among them; and three of the first horns were uprooted before it.
>
> This horn had eyes like the eyes of a man, *and a mouth that spoke boastfully.*"

The KJV says; *"...and a mouth speaking great things".*

This same description is rehearsed by Paul speaking of the Antichrist in 2 Thessalonians 2:4:

> "Who opposeth and exalteth himself above all that is called God, or that that is worshipped; so that he as God sitteth in the Temple of God showing himself that he is God." 2 Thess 2:4 (KJV)

He will be the most powerful and charismatic political leader ever to take office. Clarence Larkin in his book, Dispensational Truths, published in 1920, says of this man;

> "He will be a composite man. One who embraces in his character the abilities of Nebuchadnezzar, Alexander the Great and Caesar Augustus. He will have the marvellous gift of attracting unregenerate men. And the irresistible fascination of his personality, his versatile attainments, superhuman wisdom, great administrative and executive ability, along with his powers as a consummate flatterer, a brilliant diplomatist, a superb strategist, will make him the most conspicuous and prominent of men. All these gifts will be conferred on him by Satan, whose tool he will be."

I bet he will be better looking than Sean Connery, Elvis and George Clooney put together and the women will love him. To quote an old Irish saying, he will be able to charm the birds off a tree.

But who is this man and from whence does he come? Is he a human who is now being groomed by Satan to step into the limelight in a short time when his moment arrives? Have we seen him on TV and is he known to us? A well known politician from the EU or a rising star in US politics perhaps? Or an Arab prince who is Oxford educated and speaks nine languages fluently and has oil wealth beyond our wildest dreams?

No. He is none of these. For who he is and where he abides is clearly given in plain speech in scripture. And he will not be seen by any human eye until after the 'falling away'. Then and only then will the man of sin be revealed.

# CHAPTER 4
# The Spirits in Prison

SPECULATION AS TO THE identity of the Antichrist often appears in writings or talks given by experts in the field of eschatology. Eschatology is the technical name for the study of End Times Bible prophecy. Just about everyone thinks that the Antichrist is a human being who will be possessed by Satan and rise to power and take control of the world by political means. Some scholars believe this man will emerge as the leader of the European Union (EU). Others say he will come from the combined forces of the United Nations (UN). I have even heard a noted prophecy teacher name a particular Arab leader and states with certainty that this is the man who indeed will be the Antichrist.

I am going to approach this from a totally different angle with what you might call, lateral thinking. I am going to go to certain passages in the Bible which speak of this man and I am going to take a literal interpretation of their meaning. Where it is obvious that the language is figurative or symbolic, we will endeavour to point this out and derive the correct interpretation. For, as was earlier stated, even parables have a literal meaning. Many students of prophecy look at world events and then find scriptures to validate their opinions. We shall take a contrary view. In this volume we will go to the scriptures first, and having firmly established what they say, then and only then, peruse global happenings and see if patterns are emerging which mirror the divine predictions.

This is not an easy task and as I write, I am aware of how little I know regarding many of the prophecies still hidden in the Book of Revelation and elsewhere. I do not have all the answers and neither does any other writer who teaches and studies this subject. The last man to have all the answers was evacuated out of here some 2,000 years ago and has not returned as of this writing. Now we see through a glass darkly. Now we know in part. But when he returns, then we will know and understand. But until then...

So, the first verse I want to quote in regard to discovering who the Antichrist is and where he comes from is Revelation 11:7. Two men are to appear in the time of the Apocalypse called the Two Witnesses. These are two prophets of God who speak on God's behalf and who call people to repentance. These two men are very effective at bringing people, especially the Jewish nation, back to God and to His message. As a result of this, they are despised by the Antichrist and his government. These two prophets have supernatural powers which they invoke to demonstrate the power of God to the masses. We are not provided with the names of these two witnesses. Some have guessed as to the identity of who they are and have provided names, such as Enoch and Elijah. But the Spirit has not revealed their names so we see no need to speculate here. Speaking of these two prophets who are called the two witnesses and are to come and speak on behalf of God in the coming Apocalypse, it says:

> "Now when they had finished their testimony, the beast that comes up from the Abyss will attack them and overpower and kill them. Their bodies will lie in the street of the great city, which is figuratively called Sodom and Egypt, where also their Lord was crucified." Rev 11:7,8 (NIV)

The King James renders the same verse thus;

> "And when they shall have finished their testimony, the beast that ascends out of the bottomless pit shall make war against them and shall overcome them, and kill them. And their dead bodies shall lie in the street of the great city, which spiritually is called Sodom and Egypt, where also our Lord was crucified."

These two witness will preach the Word of God and will be a thorn in the side of the Antichrist and his administration. They have the power of God and they perform miracles such as shutting up heaven so that no rain fails. If anyone tries to harm them, fire comes from their mouths and devours them (Rev 11:5).

However, the Antichrist, also known as the Beast from the Abyss or the Beast that ascends out of the bottomless pit, overcomes them and kills them. For three and a half days the people from all nations will gaze on their bodies and rejoice that these two prophets are dead. This is interesting in that in order for people from different countries to see these dead bodies in the streets of Jerusalem, they would need to be watching CNN or SKY News or some other global network. Is it not amazing that this prophecy was written almost 2000 years ago and yet is a reality in our day?

But I digress. Regarding the Antichrist, it is stated that 'the beast that comes up from the Abyss' kills them. Again, most scholars gloss over this phrase or suppose it to be symbolic. Thirty three times throughout the Book of Revelation the man we refer to as the Antichrist bears the moniker, **'the beast that comes up from the Abyss'** or **'the beast that ascends out of the bottomless pit'**. But is there more information in scripture regarding an actual location somewhere called 'the Abyss' or 'the bottomless pit'?

The first mention of this place is given in a story related in chapter eight of the Gospel of Luke. It concerns a demon-possessed man who roamed naked among the tombs near the region of the Gadarenes close to Galilee. Often this man was bound hand and feet in chains but the demons that possessed him were so great that he could break free of the fetters. It takes immense power for a man to be able to break chains like this. Yet it was not the man himself but the evil spirits that controlled him and lived in his body that could accomplish such a feat.

We pick up the story in Luke 8 and are told that when this man saw Jesus;

> "He cried out and fell down before him and with a loud voice said, "What have I to do with thee, Jesus, Son of God Most High. I beseech thee, torment me not."
>
> (For he had commanded the evil spirit to come out of him).
>
> And Jesus asked him saying; "What is thy name?" And he said, "Legion," for many demons were entered into him.
>
> And they besought him that he would not command them to go out into *the deep*." Luke 8:28-31 (KJV)

The NIV translates the last phrase thus;

> "And they begged him repeatedly not to order them to go into *the Abyss*."

The word 'deep' in the KJV is '*abussos*' in Greek from which we derive the word 'abyss'. The evil spirit and the demons that were indwelling in this man repeatedly begged Jesus not to order them into this 'Abyss'. So apparently spirits can be ordered into this place. This is borne out in both 1 and 2 Peter and Jude 6 where it talks of spirits being in prison.

"By which also he (Jesus) went and preached unto the spirits in prison, which sometimes were disobedient...in the days of Noah." 1 Peter 3:19, 20 (KJV)

When Jesus arose from the dead, he received a new spiritual body whereby he was able to pass through walls and appear and disappear at will. This new body also allowed him to travel to this place called the Abyss where he 'preached' to the spirits who are incarcerated there because of their involvement in the goings-on which occurred on earth in the days of Noah prior to the Flood.

Jesus did not preach to these spirits in order to get them saved. For they are utterly evil and beyond redemption. The Greek for 'preached' is *kerruso* which literally means he, 'heralded his triumph' over these spirits. That is, Jesus proclaimed his victory over them. This word is the same word that is used of, for instance, when a victorious Roman general would return from a foreign campaign and parade his treasures and captives and spoils of war before the citizens of Rome. So Jesus was able to show these spirits that he had risen from the dead and in doing so, his victory over them was complete. Thus he, 'heralded his triumph' over them.

"For if God spared not the angels that sinned, but cast them down to hell *(Tartarus)*, and delivered them into chains of darkness, to be reserved unto judgement." 2 Peter 2:4 (KJV)

We are given a little more information in this verse regarding these spirits. But here they are called 'angels'. The Greek word for angels is *aggelos* which means 'messenger' or 'agent'. These messengers are spirit in nature unlike us humans who are flesh and blood. Look:

"But to which of the angels said he at any time, "Sit on my right hand until I make thine enemies thy footstool?"

Are they not all *ministering spirits*, sent forth to minister to them who shall be heirs of salvation?" Hebrews 1:13,14 (KJV)

This shows clearly that those beings we call angels, are spirit in nature. As spirit beings they are not constrained by the laws of physics as we humans are. We see this throughout scripture where appearances of these messengers are recorded. Angels always appear as men and are called men. Often these spirit men have been mistaken for ordinary human beings by those who have encountered them. For they resemble men. Perhaps this accounts for those verses in Genesis which asserts that man was made in 'the image of God'.

" And God said, "Let us make man in our image, after our likeness...So God created man in His own image, in the image of God created He him, male and female, created He them." Gen 1:26,27 (KJV)

Paul reiterates this fact in 1 Cor 11:7 (KJV), where he says;

"For a man ought not indeed to cover his head, forasmuch as he is the image and glory of God."

Returning to the angels who are incarcerated in this Abyss, there is a lot of pertinent information in these verses in the epistles of Peter and we glean another few titbits in Jude 6.

"And the angels which kept not their first estate, but left their own habitation, He hath reserved in everlasting chains under darkness unto the judgement of the great day." Jude 6 (KJV)

When we parse and analyse these verses together we find that disobedient spirits or angels, which sinned in the days of Noah, after having left their first estate, which is heaven, have been incarcerated in this prison of gloomy dungeons which is also called Tartarus. This place is the same Abyss or bottomless pit that the demons begged Jesus not to send them to. After Jesus had risen from the dead, we are told that he went and preached to these selfsame spirits who caused the sin in the days on Noah. This is reiterated in Ephesians 4:9 (KJV):

> "Now that he (Jesus) ascended, what is it but that he also descended first into the lower parts of the earth."

Eureka! Now we know where this Abyss is. For when it says that Jesus **'descended into the lower parts of the earth'**, it is not talking about him being buried when he died. For his body was placed in a tomb which is above ground and which was bought for his death by his wealthy businessman friend. When Jesus rose from the dead he received a new, spiritual body which allowed him do things like pass through walls and disappear at will. It also allowed him descend into the lower parts of this earth to herald his triumph over those angels who are held there. So the Abyss is somewhere in the depths of the bowls of this earth, under our feet.

There is more truths in these passages we need to illicit. It says that this Abyss is inhabited by both spirits and angels. It is also called Tartarus. These clues are important and in the next chapter I want to examine the connection between spirits and angels in more depth. In the meantime, here is another reference to the Beast and the Abyss from Rev 17:8 (NIV).

> "The beast which you saw once was, now is not, and will come up out of the Abyss and go to his destruction."

CHAPTER 5

# Human Men Versus Spirit Men

WE HAVE LEARNED THAT the Abyss is a place of incarceration for both spirits and angels. This place is a subterranean prison which is also named Tartarus and the bottomless pit. We need to look more closely at the relationship between angels and spirits. Most people think of spirits as invisible, ethereal or ephemeral entities that haunt houses or possess demented humans. But what relation do spirits have with angels? Let us again read Hebrews 1:13,14 (KJV):

> "But to which of the angels said he at any time, sit on my right hand until I make your enemies thy footstool?
> Are they not all ministering spirits sent forth to minister for them who shall be heirs of salvation?"

The NIV makes this verse even clearer;

> "Are not all angels ministering spirits sent to serve those who will inherit salvation?"

This is referring to what we call guardian angels who minister to those of us who are saved Christians. But it also tells us that angels are spirits. In vs.7 of this same chapter we read, **'Who makes his angels spirits and his ministers a flame of fire'**. Twice in the same chapter we are told that angels are spirits.

Another clear example of this truth is given in the Book of Acts chapter 8. This is the record of Philip who was told by an angel to go and speak to a eunuch who was high up in the government of Candace, queen of Ethiopia. After teaching this man the truth regarding the resurrection, the eunuch asks to be baptized and says that he believes that Jesus is the Son of God. Here are a few clips from the story;

> 26 "And the angel of the Lord spake unto Philip saying..."
> 29 "And the Spirit said unto Philip, 'go near...'"
> 39"And when they were come up out of the water, the Spirit of the Lord caught away Philip that the eunuch saw him no more...But Philip was found at Azotus."

It was **'the angel of the Lord'** who was sent on a special mission to Philip. Immediately afterwards the same being is called a spirit - **'the spirit said unto Philip,'** while in verse 39 the same angelic messenger is called **'the spirit of the Lord'** (i.e. the spirit from or sent by the Lord), who finished his mission by catching Philip away to Azotus. Thus we speak of someone being 'spirited away'.

This again proves that angels are spirits. But what of their appearance? What do they look like? Are they little naked cherubim with bows and arrows? Or glorious beings with long blond hair and huge wings? Well for a start, 'angel' is a misleading word. It comes from the Greek, *aggelos* and a better translation would be 'messenger' or 'agent'. The same goes for the Hebrew word, *malak*, which is also translated angel. These beings are often sent to deliver news.

> "And it came to pass while he (Zacharias) executed the priest's office ... there appeared unto him a messenger (*aggelos*) of God standing at the right side of the alter.
> And the messenger said unto him, "I am Gabriel that stands in the presence of God, and I am sent to speak unto you and to show you these glad things."
> Luke 1:8,11,19 (KJV)

This same Gabriel was sent to Daniel some 500 years before this and was the one who dictated the Book of Daniel. Here Daniel relates his meeting with Gabriel;

> "Yea, while I was speaking in prayer even THE MAN Gabriel, whom I had seen in a vision…touched me about the time of the evening oblation." Dan 9:21,22 (KJV)

This informs us that Gabriel is a man. Many times in the New Testament we have these messengers appearing to people and they are always called 'men'. For instance, when the women went to dress the body of Jesus in the tomb, they were met there by two men in shining clothes who asked them, 'why seek ye the living among the dead'? And later on, just as he ascended into Heaven, it says:

> "And while they looked steadfastly toward heaven as He went up, TWO MEN stood by them in white apparel…" Acts 1:10 (KJV)

There are lots more examples of these men, who are messengers, appearing throughout the New Testament. We are even advised to be gracious to strangers as, 'some have entertained angels thereby'. In other words, people have met and interacted with men and were unaware that these men were angelic spirit beings. A prime example of this is provided in Genesis 19 with the record of two angels who visited with Lot.

> "The two angels arrived at Sodom in the evening, and Lot was sitting in the gateway of the city. When he saw them he got up to meet them and bowed down with his face to the ground.
>
> "My lords," he said, "please turn aside to your servant's house. You can wash your feet and spend the night and then go on your way early in the morning."
>
> "No," they answered, "we will spend the night in the square."

> But he insisted so strongly that they did go with him and entered his house. He prepared a meal for them... and they ate.
>
> Before they went to bed, all the men of the city of Sodom-both young and old-surrounded the house. They called to Lot, "Where are THE MEN that came to you tonight? Bring them out to us so that we can have sex with them." Gen 19: 1-5 (NIV)

It is obvious from this passage that the two angels who visited Lot looked like men. They may well have been men with outstanding features as they attracted the attentions of all the males, both young and old, of Sodom. It says that Lot washed their feet. So angels have feet that could get dirty and needed washing. It is noteworthy that these two men had appetites as they ate the meal prepared for them. In the previous chapter to this, these same two angels ate a meal prepared for them by Abraham and his wife, Sarah. Can we take it from this that angels eat food? I think so.

So these beings that we call angels are both spirit in nature and are like men in appearance. There is only one mention of female angels in the Bible and that is in Zachariah 5 where it describes them as having wings. Nowhere are we told male angels have wings. But their nature is spirit just as our nature is flesh and blood. Because they are spirit, they exist in the plain of the supernatural and can accomplish things that are beyond us as we are mere human and are constrained to the realm of the natural.

So what we can conclude is that spirits are angels and that they look like men. So when we are told that there are spirits held in gloomy dungeons in Tartarus otherwise known as the Abyss or the bottomless pit, we can say with a surety that these are angels and that they look like men.

And no wonder. For several times in the first chapters of Genesis, speaking of the creation of Adam it says:

> "This is the book of the generations of Adam. In the day that God created man, in the likeness of God, made He him; Male and female, created He them..." Gen 5:1,2 (KJV)

> "Whoever sheds man's blood by man shall his blood be shed: for in the image of God made He man." Gen 9:6 (KJV)

At one point Jesus states, **'He who has seen me has seen the Father'**. In other words, he looks like his Father. Even though God is spirit, apparently he has an image and it is that of a man. In Revelation it speaks of the Lamb sitting on the right hand of the Throne of God and this throne is surrounded by 24 other thrones occupied by 24 elders. So when it says **'let us make man in our image'**, perhaps these elders are the personages it is referring to.

Throughout Revelation the pictures that the words paint ascribe characteristics to God that are similar to those of men. For instance, the following describes God as sitting on a throne with a scroll in His right hand;

> "Then I saw in the right hand of Him who sat on the throne a scroll with writing on both sides...Then I saw a Lamb...He came and took the scroll from the right hand of Him who sat on the throne." Rev 5:1,6,7 (NIV)

Rev 22:4 tells of a future new heaven and earth and describes what it will be like when God finally arrives to share in eternity with His children. We are informed:

> "They will see His face and His name will be on their foreheads."

Thus will be fulfilled one of the promises of the Messiah from his speech called The Beatitudes when he said, **'Blessed are the**

**pure in heart, for they shall see God'**. Matt 5:8 (KJV). So the Word attributes characteristics to God that resemble those of human men. All we can do is believe what the Word says. So when we are told that some day we will see the face of God, or that God has a right hand and sits on a throne, or that He resembles His son, we must therefore conclude the God has features which resemble men. For we are made in His image.

I know some will say that God is Spirit, and that he hath no form or comeliness. But we have deduced that angels are spirits and that they look like men and are indeed called men many times. So we can say with a certainty that angels are men. Not human as we are. But men nevertheless but of a spirit nature. In doing this we are merely believing what the scriptures plainly state.

For any who wish to argue that we humans do not look like our creator, there are several verses in the NT that states that we do. James 3:9 (NIV) is one such verse.

> "With the tongue we praise the Lord and Father, and with it we curse men, who have been made in God's likeness."

We earlier quoted this next verse to prove the same point. It may be an advantage to quickly remind ourselves of what Paul wrote:

> "For a man indeed ought not to cover his head, forasmuch as he is the image and glory of God." 1 Corinthians 11:7 (KJV)

It ought to be abundantly clear from all these passages that there are two types of men described in the Bible. Ordinary humans who are flesh and blood beings are the most prevalent. But on closely examining the scriptures that pertain to the spiritual dimension and the beings that inhabit that sphere, we perceive that those beings are also called men. Time and again we are informed that we are made in God's image. His own Son said that he resembled his Father, and Jesus was a man. Angels have been mistaken as regular men. They have appetites and wear clothes. There are both good angels and evil angels. There are 24 elders seated on 24 thrones around the throne of God. Jesus sits on the right hand of his Father and took the scroll from that same right hand. And in the future, when finally we reach the new earth wherein dwells righteousness, and meet with our Father God, we will see His face. Oh, what a day that will be.

The spirits that are incarcerated in the pit of the Abyss are angels. For we have seen that angels are spirit beings. Jesus in his risen body went and made a visit to these spirit men who are locked up in the bottomless pit which is somewhere in the depth of the earth. He addressed these evil men when he descended to this place also called Tartarus. So who are these men that inhabit the bottomless pit? When it prophecies that, **'the Beast which you saw once was, now is not, and will come up out of the Abyss and go to his destruction,'** who is this Beast? When it refers to this being as a beast, I do not believe that this term provides us with a clue to his identity. I reckon 'beast' is a figure of speech in the same way as 'Lamb of God' or 'the Lion of the tribe of Judah' are figures referring to the person of Jesus.

He is neither a lamb nor a lion. But these are characteristics of his personality insofar as he is as meek as a lamb but can also be as strong and brave as a lion when the need arises. By the same token, twice in Revelation it speaks of, **'the dragon, that old serpent, which is the Devil and Satan'**. The terms **'dragon'** and **'serpent'** are figures of speech to describe the arch enemy of God. A serpent is a cunning, sly, often poisonous creature that is as cold as ice that can sneak up on you without a sound and strike with deathly results. (Have you ever looked into the eyes of a snake? There is nothing there. It is like looking into the ocean). And a dragon is a fierce monster that devours all that it encounters.

Again these are descriptions of the evil personified in the Devil as opposed to those of the Messiah. So when it talks of the Beast from the Abyss, this word is describing the personality of the being. He is a wild beast.

Revelation 9 provides us with the emergence of this being from the bottomless pit and gives us another important clue as to his bearing.

> "And the fifth angel sounded, and I saw a star fall from heaven unto the earth, and to him was given the key to the bottomless pit. And he opened the bottomless pit; and there arose a smoke out of the pit as the smoke of a great furnace; and the sun and the air were darkened by reason of the smoke of the pit."

CHAPTER 6

# Locusts, Scorpions and the Bottomless Pit

> "And a fifth angel sounded, and I saw a star fall from heaven unto the earth..." Rev 9:1 (KJV)

The stars that we see twinkling in the night sky do not fall to earth from heaven. Heaven is a particular place and is the abode of the Most High God and His son and the 24 elders plus the myriads of spirit men we call angels. It is probable that this realm called heaven is outside our solar system. That is, our world is in a sort of time-bubble. The universe we inhabit is governed by time. But God is not.

Therefore I believe that heaven and God and the heavenly host that dwells there, are outside the time-bubble universe of which earth is a part along with the billions of stars and planets and other galaxies that make up our cosmos. This is why it states in the Book of Hebrews:

> "Therefore, since we have a great high priest, who has gone through the heavens, Jesus the Son of God, let us hold firmly to the faith we profess." Heb 4:14 (NIV)

Jesus when he ascended, passed **'through the heavens'.** He left our cosmos which is governed by time, and passed through the heavens (plural) in order to arrive at the destination wherein dwells His Father and the other heavenly beings.

So when it speaks of a star 'falling from heaven to earth', it is referring to an angel falling to earth. When you see what we call a falling star, shooting across the night sky, that is not a star at all but a small body of matter known as a meteor from outer space that becomes incandescent as a result of friction with the earth's atmosphere.

Angels are often referred to in scripture as 'stars' and also as the 'heavenly host'.

> "Where were you when I laid the earth's foundation?
> Tell me, if you understand.
> Who marked off its dimensions? Surely you know.
> Who stretched a measuring line across it?
> On what were its footings set, or who laid its cornerstone?
> While the morning stars sang together and all the angels shouted for joy." Job 38:4-7 (NIV)

In the King James Version, it says the **'sons of God'** are the angels and are called the **'morning stars'.** Isaiah 14:12, speaking of another angel says; **'How you have fallen from heaven, o morning star, son of the dawn.'**

Most commentators believe this is speaking of Lucifer and his fall from grace. This is why he is called a fallen angel but here is named the morning star. By the way, Venus is the morning star and is the brightest of the stars and can still be seen early in the morning when all the other stars have vanished because of the light of the rising sun.

So when we read that John **'saw a star fall from heaven unto the earth'**, what he saw was an angel, which we know is a (spirit) man, fall from the heavenly abode to earth. Whether this fallen angel is a good one or an evil one is moot. Perhaps we can discover this later. One would presume that if this angel is a gaoler, he must have the authority of God on his side. Nevertheless he has the key to the bottomless pit otherwise known as Tartarus and the Abyss. Again, regular stars do not have keys, and cannot unlock prisons.

And when he opens the bottomless pit, **'there arose a smoke out of the pit, as of a smoke of a great furnace; and the sun and the air were darkened, by reason of the smoke of the pit'**. We will see that upon the opening of the bottomless pit, the inhabitants that have been incarcerated there are released into the earth once more. Now here's a thought. Back in 1883 a volcano blew in Indonesia called Krakutau. The smoke that arose from it was so dense that it blotted out the sun from the earth for several days. We have seen the effects a volcano can have by the disruption of the recent activity in Iceland.

If we are to take these first verses in Revelation 9 literally, and I see no reason at this point to take them otherwise, for the bottomless pit is a real place situated deep in the earth, the evil spirit men that inhabit this Abyss are literal, because Jesus went and spoke to them. Therefore the smoke that arises from this place when it is opened has to be literal too. Then it may be that this is a similar eruption as Krakutau, and that the earth will be plunged into darkness by the smoke from the Abyss. As we shall see, the spirits, or angels, who are locked up in Tartarus are now released. So it may be safe to assume that their emergence from the gloomy dungeons onto earth is preceded by the world being plunged into darkness by the black smoke of the Abyss. If this assumption is correct, then the people who dwell on earth when this happens will have another clear sign as to what is happening as their world will be engulfed in darkness by reason of the smoke from the pit of the Abyss.

> "And there came out of the smoke locusts upon the earth; and unto them was given power, as the scorpions of the earth have power." Rev 9:3 (KJV)

Whereas many students of Revelation believe these locusts and scorpions are literal, I believe that the scripture now changes from being literal to figurative. For we have already seen that Jesus went and preached to the spirits that are held in this prison. We have concluded that these spirits are angelic beings who are men. (From now on, when you read the word 'angel', the picture in your mind should be that of a man). We have noted that Satan is also called the serpent and the dragon and these names are figures of speech and thus the Beast from the Abyss is also figurative. In the same way, the terms **'locusts'** and **'scorpions'** are figures of speech relating to angelic beings who are to come out of the Abyss. Just as the scorpions of the earth have power, so too, these locusts will also be given power when they emerge from Tartarus.

To prove this point, we use a common tool for interpreting the Bible which is to examine where similar words or phrases were used before. Very often the meaning of a word or phrase is defined in its previous or first usage. In Luke chapter 10 we have the record of Jesus sending out 70 of his disciples to preach and heal in his name. (In Matt 10:16 (KJV) He says; **"Behold I send you forth as sheep in the midst of wolves: be ye therefore wise as serpents and meek as doves"**. Here we have more names of animals to describe people: sheep, wolves, serpents and doves).

Luke 10:17,18 (KJV) informs us that when the 70 disciples return with joy, they proclaim;

> "Lord, even the demons are subject unto us through your name.
>
> And he said unto them: "I beheld Satan as lightening fall from heaven."

They mention demons and Jesus says he beheld Satan as lightening fall from heaven. Here is another mention of fallen angels. I believe that this is a prophetic utterance for this scripture is still future and has yet to be fulfilled. But we will deal with that later. Listen to the next statement.

> "Behold I give you power to tread on SERPENTS and SCORPIONS and over all the power of the enemy: and nothing shall by any means hurt you.
> Notwithstanding in this rejoice not, that THE SPIRITS are subject unto you; but rather rejoice because your names are written in heaven..."

Wow, wow, wow! Back up a minute. Read these last few verses again. The disciples mention that even the demons are subject to them. Then he talks of Satan falling from heaven and tells them they have power to tread on scorpions and serpents, and over all the power of the enemy. Well who is our enemy? Who are the serpents and scorpions? He defines them in the next sentence;

> '...in this rejoice not, that the SPIRITS are subject unto you.'

So the serpents and scorpions are spirits who are our enemy according to Jesus. And we have seen that spirits are angels which are men, but of a spirit nature. So right here in these verses we are told that all these names; serpents, scorpions, lambs and wolves, are figures of speech for men. The disciples are the lambs while the wolves are their enemy which are also called serpents and scorpions. It is over these spirits that the disciples have power through the name of Jesus.

And of course the serpent, who is the dragon, is Satan and the Devil, twice so called in the Book of Revelation. Rev 12:9 (KJV), states:

> "And the dragon was cast out, that old serpent called the Devil and Satan which deceives the whole world: he was cast out into the earth and his angels were cast out with him."

This prophecy is still future and this is what Jesus was eluding to when he said, **'I beheld Satan as lightening having fallen from heaven.'** We will return to this topic later where it will be researched more fully.

It was the serpent who beguiled (seduced ) Eve in the garden and caused what has come to be known as the fall of man. Not a snake. Nor a man with a serpentine or reptilian likeness. For some conclude that these evil angels look like serpents or lizards. If you follow this logic, then perhaps they can look like dragons also!

No. **'Serpent'** and **'dragon'** are figures of speech for Satan who is the Devil. And he no more looks like a snake or a dragon as Jesus looks like a lamb or a lion. These names of animals are given as figures and also describe the personality of those to which they appertain. Thus we have lion and lamb referring to Jesus. The serpent and dragon who is Satan. The Beast from the Abyss who is the Antichrist. Lambs among wolves talking of the disciples among demons. And scorpions and locusts referring to spirits. The locusts are the spirit men who will come out of the bottomless pit and they will be given power even as the scorpions (evil fallen angels) have presently got power on this earth (Rev 9:3).

So these locusts and scorpions are as serpents and are men: spirit men or angels who are evil and who will be manifest on the earth once again as they were prior to the Flood of Noah. What these fallen angels did prior to the Flood which necessitated them being locked up in Tartarus, will be discussed in due course. That these locusts and scorpions are spirit beings is provable in another verse further down in this same chapter nine of Revelation and I will deal with this in the next chapter. But why call these spirits **'locusts'** and **'scorpions'**? Well think about it. What are the characteristics of locusts? To begin with, locusts wipe out everything in their path. As they descend and attack an area, everything is destroyed. Devastation is left in their wake. Then they move on to the next patch. Meanwhile the sting from a scorpion usually means vicious pain and torture or instant death. Thus these evil fallen angels, spirit men who are to inhabit the earth during the Apocalypse, are vile serpents, scorpions and locusts. Woe unto the inhabitants of the earth when this becomes a reality.

CHAPTER 7

# The Antichrist Exposed and Named

THE BOTTOMLESS PIT HAS now been opened by an angel that has fallen to earth from heaven bearing a key. The angels that have been incarcerated in this prison are released onto the earth and are given power.

Before we identify who the actual Antichrist is and name him, I want to reiterate an important point. It is imperative that we allow the words in scripture to sketch on the canvass of our minds the picture it presents. We must put aside our previous beliefs, notions and ideas and let the Word interpret itself in order to acquire the true meaning of what we read. Thus, with the guidance of the Spirit of Truth, we may be able to glean some of the certainties regarding what is coming upon the world and humankind in the near future.

With this in mind, we must remove from our psyche the idea that angels resemble either naked cherubim with small wings or men with huge wings. This is not the picture that scripture paints. These images have come down through the centuries from various artists and no doubt have been inspired by Satan in order to deceive us. Instead we look at what the Bible has to say regarding angels and we form pictures in our mind from the words we read there.

And it portrays angels as men. So every time now that we read the word 'angel,' we think of men. It was two men who walked into Sodom back in Genesis 19. And they must have been attractive men as all the men of Sodom wanted to fulfill their evil desires with them. People have entertained angels unaware. These angels so resembled men that the folks that entertained them did not know that they were actual spirit men; angels.

That they are good-looking men seems logical as angels are created spirit beings and are called in scripture, sons of God. So it follows that His creation would be beautiful beings. And I would venture that even the evil angels are very attractive men. For, as we shall see, it was attractive and irresistible supernatural men that fell to earth 1,000 years or so before the Flood of Noah and seduced the human women of that bygone era.

These are the angels who have been locked up in the Abyss because of their sin in the days of Noah. These men are fallen angels and are the Nephilim mentioned in Genesis chapter 6. We will return to this topic presently, but for now let us pick up again the story of the opening of the bottomless pit and the release of the angels who are called locusts in Revelation 9. The actual identity of the man we call the Antichrist is given here and most scholars have totally missed this truth even though it is written in plain language right under our very noses. But just before I reveal the identity of the Antichrist to you, I want to emphasise again to you the need to stick to what the Word declares and not be distracted by what man says. To do this we listen to a lesson from the Master Teacher Himself given in Matthew 16. Here Jesus asked His disciples, who do people think I am?

> "And they said, "Some say thou art John the Baptist: some Elias and some, Jeremiah, or one of the prophets."
> He said to them, "But whom say you that I am?"

> And Peter answered and said, "Thou art the Christ, the Son of the living God."
> And Jesus said unto him, "Blessed art thou, Simon Bar-jona, for flesh and blood hath not revealed it unto thee, But my Father which is in heaven..."
> From that time forth began Jesus to show unto His disciples how that He must go unto Jerusalem, and suffer many things of the elders and chief priests and scribes and be killed and be raised again the third day.
> Then Peter took him and began to rebuke him saying, "Be it far from thee Lord: this shall not be unto thee."
> But he turned and said unto Peter, "Get thee behind me Satan, for thou art an offence unto me: for thou savourest not the things that be of God, but those that be of men." Matt 16:14-17, 21-23 (KJV)

This is an important lesson we need to grasp going forward. Jesus asked his disciples who did they think he was. Peter gave the correct answer and Jesus praised him and told him it was by way of revelation from God Himself that Peter had received this knowledge. Then Jesus began to tell them that he must fulfil prophecy by going to Jerusalem and suffering at the hands of the religious leaders and die before being raised from the dead.

At this Peter lost the run of himself and more or less said, 'No way is this going to happen while I am around to protect you...' Then Jesus looked Peter square in the eyes and said, 'Get thee behind me Satan, you are nothing but a snare to me. You only regard the things of men and not the things of God...'

Whew! What a turnaround. One minute Peter was cock-of-the-walk because Jesus had praised him for his spiritual insight and had given him the keys of the kingdom. Next thing he hits him right between the eyes with, 'Satan is working through you...you are more interested in man's opinions than the Word of God..', or words to that effect. So Peter went from hero to zero in just a couple of minutes.

The lesson here is, the way of truth is a very narrow path. Jesus was the Word made flesh. He spoke the Word of truth because He was truth. So when he began to explain to his disciples what had to come to pass in order that man's redemption could be attained, he was speaking God's truth. But when Peter reacted as he did, he was using his five senses and was going directly against the revealed Word of truth. Thus he was stepping off the narrow path and into error.

As soon as one starts to stray from the simple teaching of scripture, and begins to put forth ones own opinion, then you are making the same mistake that Peter made and the Lord's rebuke might be the same to you: 'Get you behind me Satan'. For now you have strayed off the narrow path of truth and are perpetrating half-truths or speculation which, if we are to take Jesus at face value, are satanic in nature.

I say this because now we are going to go to the Word and it is going to reveal to us the truth regarding the name of the Antichrist and his present abode. All other opinions are void. This information is in this next verse. Listen:

> "And they had a KING over them which is the ANGEL of the bottomless pit, whose name in the Hebrew tongue is Abaddon but in the Greek tongue hath his name Apollyon." Rev. 9:11(KJV)

This is the name of he whom is called the Beast from the Abyss 33 times in Revelation and he is both an **angel** and a **king**. Abaddon and Apollyon.

So here we have it. The name of the Antichrist and his whereabouts is clearly given in simple language right here in verse eleven. This secret has been hidden in plain sight right before our eyes for almost 2,000 years, yet practically no one has spotted it. Multitudes of researchers and scholars and authors and prophecy teachers have been speculating on the identity of the Antichrist for many years, and they are all wrong. You are blessed that the Lord has revealed this mystery to you which has been hidden for centuries.

That the name of the Antichrist is here provided for all to see, is an amazing and momentous revelation, in my opinion. For now all doubt is removed. No more can Christians point at some human politician and say, 'he is the Antichrist'. For his name is Abaddon and Apollyon and he is both an angel and a king and he is presently locked up in Tartarus, awaiting the opening of the bottomless pit.

But an angel is a man. So this person who is to appear on the world stage in the coming Apocalypse and take control of the world is a man. A spirit man who is an evil angel who has been incarcerated in the Abyss since the time of the Flood of Noah some 4,350 years ago. His name is Abaddon in Hebrew and in Greek is Apollyon. The Destroyer. It is because he is a spiritual being endued with supernatural abilities, that he can perform 'signs, miracles and wonders' and deceive the whole world thereby. No ordinary flesh and blood human could perform such feats.

But here is the thing. Apollyon is how the Greeks spell 'Apollo'. And Apollo is one of the original leaders of the gods of Greek and Roman mythology who reigned at Olympus some thousands of years ago along with the other so-called gods, namely; Mars, Saturn, Zeus, Mercury, Poseidon, Jupiter, Sirius, Venus, Orion etc. Interestingly, there were some female goddesses also; Hera, Demeter and Athena (of which Athens is named after). In ancient mythology, Apollo is described as being the epitome of the beauty of man. He was the god of music and prophecy and medicine. His oracle was at Delphi in Greece and this remains today as an amazing structure and a huge tourist attraction. But temples to Apollo are scattered all over Greece and Turkey and that whole area. For Apollo was a revered leader of the ancient gods of legend.

Most learned persons suppose that Apollo and the rest of the Olympian gods are mere flights of fancy and dismiss them as myths. But we are not dealing in myths or fables. Our studies are to do with the revealed Word of truth and Holy Writ. And it testifies that Apollo is an angelic man who is locked up in Tartarus because of his role in the sin and violence that pertained in the days of Noah that precipitated the Flood in those bygone eras. So the legends which talk of gods on the earth in ancient times may not be the myths that we were led to believe they were. In fact, the more we delve into the mythologies of yore and place them alongside the ancient scriptures, the more we see how much these stories parallel each other.

The other truth we must note well in this verse which speaks of Apollo, is that he is called here a 'king'. This is vitally important as we advance this investigation into the hidden prophecies of the Apocalypse. For we must allow the scriptures define the concepts we ponder so that the right picture emerges which will in turn provide the proper interpretation regarding the message. In this regard the fact that Apollo is here called a king is a very telling truth. For we will be examining other verses which talk of kings and we must accept that these other kings are of the same ilk as Apollo if we agree that the scriptures are the only template whereby the Word can interpret itself to us.

The Nephilim are mentioned first in Genesis 6:4 (NIV).

> " When men began to increase in number on the earth and daughters were born to them, the sons of God saw the daughters of men were beautiful, and they married any of them they chose.
>
> The Nephilim were on the earth in those days-and also afterwards-when the sons of God went to the daughters of men and had children by them. They were the heroes of old, men of renown."

'Nephilim' is a Hebrew word which means, 'the fallen ones'. Some Hebrew scholars insist the these Nephilim were the off-spring of the fallen angels and were giants. But the majority of Hebrew scholars agree that this word literally means 'the fallen ones'. In the context of the many other places in scripture which speaks of angels falling from heaven to earth, it seems clear that the original Nephilim are the sons of God who fell from grace, fell from heaven and fell to earth, and then had sex with human women who bore children to them.

Verse four also says that these fallen angels were on the earth in the days of Noah, **'and also afterwards'**. That is, there was a second irruption of Nephilim with humans some time *after* the Flood. More on this later.

The expression, **'sons of God'**, occurs eight times in the Old Testament. It is clear from all eight that the phrase **'sons of God'** is referring to created spirit beings, namely, angels. We have already looked at one passage from Job 38:7. Here are two more:

> "Now there was a day when the sons of God came to present themselves before the Lord, and Satan came also among them." Job 1:6 (KJV)

Satan was a holy son of God before his revolt and here we see him assembling with other angels to appear before God.

Daniel chapter 3 provides the story of three servants of God, Meshach, Shadrach and Abednego, who, because of their stand for God, were thrown into a burning furnace. But the king, on looking into the fire states:

> "Lo, I see four men walking in the midst of the fire… and the form of the fourth is like the son of God."

In the KJV, it translates the last phrase, **'…the form of the fourth is like THE son of God'**. But there is no article 'the' in the Hebrew text. Therefore it should read; 'a' son of God. That is, a supernatural being or an angel. When the king addresses the three men after they are delivered from the fire, he says:

> "Blessed be the God of Mesach, Shadrach and Abed-nego, who hath sent HIS ANGEL and delivered his servants..." Dan 3: 25, 28 (KJV)

There are some who continue to insist that the sons of God are not angels but are humans from the line of Seth or someone else. But as workmen of the Word we must be honest with ourselves and with others. On reading all eight passages where these occur it is clear that **'sons of God'** are angels. Created spirit beings. (For those with a copy of EW Bullinger's, *The Companion Bible,* I refer you to Appendix 23 entitled, 'The sons of God in Gen 6', which provides a detailed study on this topic. This edition is also available on-line).

The offspring of these fallen angels were the giants of the Old Testament and of numerous traditions and historical accounts from all over the world. The Genesis record also squares with the so-called mythologies from many traditions which speak of gods descending to earth from heaven and taking mortal women to wife who in turn bare children to them. These traditions are well documented in Greek and Roman writings as well as the Egyptian writings such as The Pyramid Texts and the Egyptian Book of the Dead. Other traditions, from South America to the Far East, testify to these truths and speak of gods descending to earth from heaven and copulating with women and fathering children.

In Appendix 25 of his seminal book, *The Companion Bible,* EW Bullinger, writing of these Nephilim says:

> "We have in these mighty men, the "men of renown", the explanation of the origin of the Greek mythology. That mythology was no mere invention of the human brain, but it grew out of the traditions and memories and legends of the doings of that mighty race of beings; and was gradually evolved out of the

> "heroes" of Gen 6. The fact that they were supernatural in their origin formed an easy step to being regarded as the demi-gods of the Greeks.
>
> Thus the Babylon "Creation Tablets", the Egyptian "Book of the Dead", the Greek mythology and heathen cosmogonies, which by some are set on an equality with scripture, or by others adduced in support of it, are all the corruption and perversion of primitive truths, distorted in proportion as their origin was forgotten, and their memories faded away."

The Book of Enoch is a most ancient book which was discovered with other writings among the Dead Sea Scrolls. Experts tell us these scrolls were placed in the cave where they were hidden, circa 300BC. Although few people of the Christian faith are aware of this book, the early founding fathers of the Church regarded it as being divinely inspired and included it in the Canon of Scripture. It was only removed at a much later date. The Book of Enoch fills in many of the blanks pertaining to the days prior to the Flood which are not covered in scripture. Jude, who was the brother of Jesus, quotes directly from the Book of Enoch in his epistle. It is safe to presume that if the brother of Jesus knew of the writings of Enoch, then so did the rest of the Apostles and they probably discussed this with Jesus himself while he was still with them.

This confirms that we can research the testimony of Enoch with a degree of certainty that his writings can be trusted. If it were otherwise, then in no way would he be quoted in the divinely inspired Word of God by the brother of Jesus. So what does Enoch have to say of fallen angels coming to earth and having sexual relations with human women? And does he also name the leader of these angels whom we can associate with the one which scripture defines as the Antichrist; Apollo of Revelation? We shall return to this topic at some length later in this thesis.

CHAPTER 8

# Uncovered: The Seven Heads and Ten Horns

SCRIPTURE INTERPRETS SCRIPTURE. THIS should be the mantra for all students of the Bible. This way it is not left to one's own interpretation. We have been studying a person called the beast from the Abyss. It has been deduced that his name is Apollo which appears in Revelation 9:11 as Apollyon which is the Greek spelling. In Hebrew he is named Abaddon.

We are told that he is both an angel and that he is the king of those other angels who reside in the Abyss with him at present.

> "The beast that thou sawest was, and is not; shall ascend out of the bottomless pit, and go into perdition: And they that dwell on the earth shall wonder, whose names are not written in the book of life from the foundation of the world, when they behold the beast that was, and is not, and yet is." Rev 17: 8 (KJV)

When it says here that the beast shall ascend out of the bottomless pit, **'and go into perdition'**, this means he will go into destruction or ruin. A cursory reading of this passage suggests that the Antichrist will go into ruin or be destroyed. But that is not the proper rendering. What it is saying is, that he, the Antichrist or Apollo, will set about destroying the world.

The NIV gives it thus:

> "The beast which you saw once was, now is not, and will come up out of the Abyss and go to his destruction."

That is, he will proceed to cause such havoc so as to destroy the world and its inhabitants. Thus his name; 'the Destroyer'.

Revelation 11 tells of the two witnesses who preach and prophesy for God and if any man hurts them; **'fire proceeds out of their mouths and devour their enemies...'** These two prophets are powerful preachers who will turn many people to God in these future days. After three and a half years, they are killed by the Antichrist.

> "And when they shall have finished their testimony, the beast that ascends out of the bottomless pit shall make war against them and overcome them and kill them Rev 11: 7 (KJV)

Apollo, **'the beast from the Abyss'**, as the all-powerful Antichrist, has the wherewithal to kill the two witnesses of God. Revelation 13 provides several facts concerning this coming being. It begins;

> "And the dragon (Satan) stood on the shore of the sea. And I saw a beast coming out of the sea. He had ten horns and seven heads, with ten crowns on his horns...The beast I saw resembled a leopard, but had feet like those of a bear and a mouth like that of a lion.
>
> The dragon gave the beast his power and his throne and great authority. One of the heads of the beast seemed to have had a fatal wound, but the fatal wound had been healed." Rev 13:1-3 (NIV)

Fatal means dead. So he was dead, perhaps assassinated, and raised from death. As was already stated, Satan always copies or duplicates what the true God does. So here we have a counterfeit resurrection of the Antichrist designed to deceive the majority of the blind multitudes who are able to view these happenings via global TV. As a result;

> "The whole world was astonished and followed the beast. Men worshipped the dragon, because he had given authority to the beast. They also worshipped the beast..."
> Rev 13:3,4

But what are these ten horns and seven heads? Some scholars have taken these words as literal and produced hideous pictures of ridiculous looking multi-headed monsters emerging from the sea. But our mantra is, scripture interprets scripture. With this in mind we jump to chapter 17:3,7 (NIV) where these metaphors are explained.

> "Then the angel carried me away in the Spirit into a desert. There I saw a woman sitting on a scarlet beast that was covered with blasphemous names and had seven heads and ten horns.
>
> Then the angel said to me, "Why are you astonished? I will explain to you the mystery of the woman and of the beast she rides, which has the seven heads and ten horns."

This now takes all the guesswork out of it and we are not left to man's ideas or interpretations as to what he thinks this passage may be saying. For the Spirit is now going to explain the true interpretation which means we do not have to trust in ordinary humans to figure out what it means.

> "The beast which you saw once was, now is not, and will come up out of the Abyss and go to his destruction. The inhabitants of the earth whose names have

> not been written in the book of life from the creation of the world will be astonished when they see the beast because he once was, now is not, and yet will come." Rev 17:8 (NIV)

Because we have identified the beast from the Abyss as being an angel or spirit man whose name is Apollo, this passage is not difficult. For Apollo was a god of legend who was a fallen angel or Nephilim, who, because of his sin in causing the violence and bloodshed in the days prior to the Flood, is incarcerated in the Abyss to be released in this future time. This is why the scripture says he:

**"Once was..."** In the 1,000 years or so when he reigned with the other gods or fallen angels of yore prior to the Flood of Noah.

**"Now is not..."** Because he is locked up in Tartarus no longer free to roam.

**"And will come up out of the Abyss and go to his destruction..."** In the near coming Apocalypse when the Pit is opened and he ascends to take his role as the all-powerful Antichrist which will end in the destruction of almost the whole world.

We are left in no doubt as to who the beast is. He is called elsewhere, the man of sin. The son of perdition. The man of lawlessness. He is a man whose nature is spirit as is the nature of all the angels so called. We read on.

> "The seven heads are seven hills on which the woman sits. THEY ARE ALSO SEVEN KINGS." Rev 17:9,10 (NIV)

As Apollo is described as an angel and king who rules over the rest of the angels of the Abyss, so these seven other kings must also be angels or spirit men just as the god of the Abyss, Apollo, is. For we are implicitly told here that the 'seven heads' are 'seven kings'. A king is a ruler of people.

It does not state that they are seven 'kingdoms'. A kingdom is not a king. Many have taken the liberty of making these kings into countries that they insist are invariably Muslim countries in the Middle East. No. All the confusion and all the divergent opinions on this chapter arise from ignoring this simple fact, and from looking at these individuals as kingdoms instead of 'kings'. That is contrary to the explanation given to John by the angel who says that the seven heads are seven kings. They are kings just as Apollo is a king which means they are Nephilim which are fallen angels. In fact, the next verse confirms this. Speaking of these seven kings it says:

> " Five have fallen, one is, the other has not yet come..." Rev 17:10 (NIV)

As the star (angel) with the key to the bottomless pit 'fell' to earth; as the stars (angels) of heaven 'fell' to earth like figs falling from a fig tree; and as Jesus prophetically saw Satan 'having fallen' like lightening from heaven, so too, these are 'fallen' angels who are to be kings in the near coming Apocalypse who will be under the power of the Antichrist who in turn is under the power of the dragon who is the serpent, the Devil and Satan, the greatest of all the fallen angels.

We are told, **'five have fallen, one is, the other has not yet come...'** Does this mean that five angels had already fallen at the time John wrote Revelation, or are they to fall to earth at some future point during the Apocalypse? We cannot say. My hunch is that five of these seven kings had already fallen to earth at the time of the writing. Perhaps they were part of the band that fell to earth and mated with human women for the second time, after the Flood?

When it says, **'...one is, the other has not yet come,'** we reckon that one of these kings refers to Apollo. For we are also told that the beast from the Abyss, **'..is an eighth king, but belongs to the seven'**. He is called an eighth 'king', not an eighth 'head'. The Spirit then tell us who the ten horns are:

> "And the ten horns that thou sawest are ten kings, who have not yet received a kingdom; but they receive authority as kings at one and the same hour as the Beast." Rev 17:12 (KJV)

We are not to re-interpret His interpretation. It is plainly stated that the seven heads are seven kings. Likewise we are informed that the ten horns are ten kings. This makes a total of seventeen kings who will have as their leader the angel of the Abyss, Apollo. So all these seventeen kings are spirit men who are to come in the future. Ten will receive kingdoms in the future and will be subject to the Antichrist who is the Destroyer. He in turn receives his power from the dragon (Satan), and is subject to him.

The False Prophet is mentioned three times in Revelation (16:13, 19:20, and 20:10).

> "And I saw another beast coming up out of the earth and he had two horns like a lamb." Rev 16:13 (KJV)

We can apply the same rule here pertaining to what the two horns are and conclude that they are also kings. Along with the False Prophet this makes three more kings or fallen angels who are to appear on the world stage along with the other seventeen. That makes a total of twenty fallen angels who will be prominent in ruling the world when this prophecy is realised. Coincidentally, in the Book of Enoch it records that 200 Watchers fell to earth and mated with human women originally. Enoch provides the names of their leaders and they are twenty in number. Enoch gives the name of their commander as Azazel.

The three main leaders who are to deceive almost the whole world are now named. We have the False Prophet who works on behalf of the Antichrist who receives his power from the dragon who is the Devil. This is an infernal Trinity and a direct counterfeit and opposition to Jesus Christ, the Holy Spirit and God the Most High.

CHAPTER 9

# The 10 Super Nation States of the New World Order

IN ORDER TO MAKE sense of who these ten kings are and what they represent, we must go back to the Book of Daniel, written circa 495BC, some 2,500 years ago, which provides additional information regarding what is to happen during the Apocalypse.

Daniel had several visions concerning the End Times which much troubled him. In chapter 7:2-8 (KJV), he records one vision he had regarding four great empires which were to come after his death. The fourth was referring to the government which will emerge in the time of the Antichrist.

> "Daniel spake and said, "I saw in my vision by night and behold the four winds of the heaven strove upon the great sea.
>
> And four great beasts came up from the sea, diverse one from another.
>
> The first was like a lion, and had eagle's wings...
>
> And behold another beast, a second like to a bear, and it raised up itself on one side, and it had three ribs in the mouth of it between the teeth of it...

After this I beheld, and lo another, like a leopard, which had upon the back of it four wings of a fowl; the beast had also four heads; and dominion was given to it.

After this I saw in the night visions, and behold a fourth beast, dreadful and terrible and strong exceedingly; and it had great iron teeth: it devoured and brake in pieces and stamped the residue with the feet of it: it was diverse from all the beasts that were before it; and it had ten horns.

I considered the ten horns, and behold, there came up among them another little horn...and behold in this horn were eyes like the eyes of a man, and a mouth speaking great things."

This **'little horn'** is another name for the Antichrist. His description here concurs with that given by the apostle Paul in 2 Thessalonians 2:3,4 (KJV).

"Let no man deceive you by any means: for that day shall not come except there come a falling away first, and that man of sin be revealed, the son of perdition,

Who opposeth and exalteth himself above all that is called God, or that is worshipped; so that he as God sitteth in the Temple of God, shewing himself that he is God."

And we see the fulfilment of these prophecies in Revelation 13:5,6 (KJV). Speaking of the **'beast that rises from the sea'** it says:

"And there was given unto him a mouth speaking great things and blasphemes...And he opened his mouth in blasphemy against God to blaspheme His name, and His tabernacle and them that dwell in heaven."

So the 'little horn' is the Antichrist. Dan 7:24 explains of the other ten horns.

> 'And the ten horns out of this kingdom are TEN KINGS that shall arise...'

This proves beyond all doubt that these ten kings are just that; kings. It does not say they are 'ten kingdoms'. The little horn is the Antichrist who is the king and Beast from the Abyss and the other ten horns are ten other kings who will reign with him in this future 'kingdom' which will be a world-wide, one-world government. As recorded in the Book of Revelation, these kings are to 'arise out of the sea'. This is another clue as to the location of the Abyss or Tartarus. It is beneath the sea. Possibly the Mediterranean sea.

I say this because of a boating experience some friends of mine had off the southern tip of Greece a couple of years back. While sailing in this spot, they were hit by a ferocious storm so they headed for the nearest harbour for shelter. After vying with the storm for some time, they made it in safely and docked. While sitting out the gale, they got chatting to some locals who informed them that, according to local legend, the opening to Tartarus was under the sea just off the southern coast. This is why I surmise that the sea mentioned might be the Mediterranean.

More information on this coming government is provided in chapter two of Daniel which records his interpretation of a dream which the then king, Nebuchadnezzar, had. In this dream Nebuchadnezzar saw a huge statue made up of different substances. Daniel explained what the king saw:

> "The image's head was of fine gold, his breast and his arms of silver, his belly and his thighs of brass.
> His legs of iron, his feet part of iron and part of clay."
> Dan 2:32,33 (KJV)

Daniel then explains that the 'head of gold' was the empire of Nebuchadnezzer himself. This was superseded by the 'breast and arms of silver' which was the Medo-Persian empire which in turn was to be followed by the empire of Alexander the Great which was the 'belly and thighs of brass'. The 'legs of iron' referred to the mighty Roman Empire. All these empires came to pass in the centuries that followed.

Then Daniel speaks of a fifth world dominion which was to come in the far distant future. He described this empire as having ten toes made of both iron and clay (Dan 2:41-45 KJV).

> "And whereas thou sawest the feet and toes, part of potters clay and part of iron, the kingdom shall be divided; but there shall be in it the strength of the iron, forasmuch as thou saw the iron mixed with the miry clay.
>
> And as the toes of the feet were part of iron and part of clay, so the kingdom shall be partly strong and partly broken (fragile).
>
> And whereas thou sawest iron mixed with miry clay, THEY SHALL MINGLE THEMSELVES WITH THE SEED OF MEN; but they shall not cleave one to another, even as iron is not mixed with clay.
>
> And in the days of THESE KINGS shall the God of heaven set up a kingdom which shall never be destroyed..."

In this we have the Old Testament prophecy of the fulfilment of the events we have recently been discussing. That is, the ten toes are the ten horns which are the ten kings who are under the power and authority of the Antichrist in the coming one-world government of the New World Order. The word 'kings' means rulers. In our day these kings might be Prime Ministers or Presidents or heads of the ten supra-nation states that are to come.

Daniel states that the ten toes are made partly of iron and partly of clay. He also says, **'they shall mingle themselves with the seed of men'** (Dan 2:43 KJV). This hint leads us to believe that this section is referring to the Nephilim mingling with humans in order to rule the world.

We humans are the clay; **'Dust thou art and unto dust thou shalt return'**. But the fallen angels are like the strength of iron as compared to us humans which are mere clay, for they are supernatural and superhuman in nature having great spiritual powers at their disposal. Therefore the Antichrist will reign over a world-wide government consisting of ten geo-political supra-nation states who will in turn be ruled by fallen angels together with human politicians. Iron and clay.

The Roman Empire ruled most of the world in the centuries both before and after the time of Christ. This was represented by the 'legs of iron' in the dream. And the empire of the Antichrist is made up of toes of both iron and clay. This has lead many commentators to deduce that the Antichrist therefore must come out of Europe as that is where the original Roman Empire hailed from. They also conclude that the Antichrist may well be the leader of the European Union. This view was especially valid when there was ten members in the EU.

However, now there are 27 countries in the EU and more are lined up to join. We must also take note that in Revelation it states several times that the Antichrist is to rule the whole world and not just 10 nations in Europe. For instance, Rev 13:8 (KJV):

> " And ALL that dwell upon the earth shall worship him, whose names are not written in the book of life of the Lamb slain from the foundation of the world."

So these ten regions under the rule of the Antichrist is a world-wide organisation. Also, any future military, economic and political union will have to have the United States of America as a pre-eminent member. This in no way contradicts the prophecy of the ten toes as being connected to the Roman Empire. For if we look at the different ethnic mixes that make up the peoples of the USA, then the vast majority of them have their roots in Europe. So one could say that the USA is, by extension, related to the old Roman Empire.

Is there any indication in world events today that the global political scene is heading in the direction of a one-world government? I think there is. For instance, in June of 2008 the Irish voted 'No' in a referendum on what is called the Lisbon Treaty. This treaty is designed to bring all 27 countries of the EU together in a political alliance with its own President and Foreign Minister. This new EU would be a sort of Federal United States of Europe with its own military.

All 27 countries have to ratify this treaty in order for it to be passed into law. Although the peoples of both France and Holland rejected this same Constitution just a few years ago in their own referenda, the political elites pressed ahead undeterred. But the Irish 'No' vote has thrown a spanner in the works.

Despite this, I predict that the EU power elites will insist on ratification by all the other 26 countries and the Irish will have to vote again in a second referendum and next time they must do as their political masters tell them to do and vote 'Yes'. I believe this because I know that the 'powers that be' are already setting in place the plans which will suit the setting up of the New World Order or One World government that is prophesied in Holy Writ. The European Union will be one of these ten regions under the power and authority of the coming Antichrist.

(Since writing the above, there has already been a second referendum in Ireland in 2009 and a 'Yes' vote was returned. Plans to set up the New World Order continue unabated).

In the same way we hear of an alliance between Mexico, Canada and the United States of America. It is called the North American Free Trade Alliance or NAFTA for short. A new currency called the Amero is said to be introduced and the union may be called the American United States. This seems to be a done deal despite the protestations of many of the citizens of these countries. But in the USA as in the EU, democracy is ignored and the will of the political elites takes precedence.

Similar alliances are taking place in South America and elsewhere. Because of the recent financial meltdown world-wide, 20 countries convened at a meeting in Washington DC. TV pictures showed the delegates from all these countries seated in a large room. In front of these delegates, emblazoned on the carpet in huge letters was the slogan, 'One World Economy'. Everywhere now you will hear politicians speak of a 'New World Order' which must come about if we are to tackle and overcome the major problems that are facing the world. The political elites that are pushing this agenda often use the excuse of global warming as a means to further their objectives.

With regard to the entire world being divided into ten sections, I recently learned that the UN already have the world split up into ten regions that may be the template for the coming ten rulers who have not yet received their kingdoms.

So yes. It appears that the world is already being prepared for the advent of the man of sin, the political leader who is to arise on the world stage after the departure of the Church of God, and take control along with his ten lieutenants. But as iron and clay do not mix, so there will be trouble and dispute between the humans and the spirit men in the governance of these ten Super Nation states. What nature these disputes will take we cannot say. But there will be discord.

As to the seven heads and who they are and what role they play, again this is not clear. We already have the G-7 made up of the leaders of the seven richest countries in the world. Also there is the seven permanent members of the United Nations. Perhaps there will be a new club set up to facilitate the imposition of this coming government and this may be under the auspices of NATO (North Atlantic Treaty Association).

We are not given the names of the seven heads who are seven rulers, except for Apollo. And it is doubtful he will go by this name when he arrives to rule as he will present himself as Christ. But there are astronomical connections with many of the gods named in legends and scripture which may provide clues as to who these other seven are. I have detailed the connections between gods so-called and heavenly bodies in my book, *The Nephilim and the Pyramid of the Apocalypse.*

Suffice to say that many of the prominent characters in scripture bare the names of stars and planets. For instance, Leo is connected with the Lion of the tribe of Judah referring to Jesus. Virgo is the sign of the virgin, who is Mary. Draco is a constellation close to another called Serpens and both these refer to the dragon and the serpent who is the devil. Likewise Apollo is a planet and in scripture angels, both good and evil, are often referred to as the 'host of heaven' or stars. Lucifer is connected to Venus, 'the bright and morning star'.

So who are the seven heads which are seven kings or rulers and seven fallen angels to be revealed in due course? Can we speculate as to who they may be? Perhaps the seven days of the week may provide us with some clues. For each of the seven days are named after seven gods who are also seven planets. The Greeks called the days of the week *Theon hemerai* which means, 'days of the gods'.

Sunday is the first day of the week. In Greek it is *helios* which means 'sun god' and is described as being associated with the god Apollo.

Monday is named after the Moon. Artemis is a goddess linked to the moon.

Tuesday is named after the god of war, Mars.

Wednesday means Mercury's day.

Thursday is named after Jupiter.

Friday is Venus or Aphrodite: a goddess of sex. Perhaps this is related to the 'Queen of heaven' mentioned in scripture?

Saturday is associated with the god, Saturn. He gave his name to the Roman festival of *Saturnalia* which was a drunken feast and orgy of revelry.

Thus we have the gods, Apollo, Moon (?), Mars, Mercury, Jupiter, Venus and Saturn.

Mars is known as the god of war and is referred to as 'the red planet'. In Roman mythology he is said to be the father of Romulus, the founder of Rome. The opening of the first four seals provide us with the four horsemen of the Apocalypse. The first rider is on a white horse. This is the Antichrist whom we have identified as the god Apollo. Next we have the rider on the red horse. Rev 6:4 (KJV):

> "And there went out another horse that was red: and power was given to him that sat thereon to take peace from the earth, and that they should kill one another: and there was given unto him a great sword."

**'Wars and rumours of wars'** was prophesied by Jesus as a significant factor of the Apocalypse. It is obvious that this particular rider is responsible for the wars that are to occur. He is riding a red horse and Mars is known as the red planet and the god of war. Perhaps we have now identified this individual as the god Mars who reigned along with Apollo in the pre Flood era. His position in the coming one world government may be that of Security Minister.

By the same token, let us look at the rider on the black horse:

> "When the Lamb opened the third seal, I heard the third living creature say, "Come". I looked and there before me was a black horse. Its rider was holding a pair of scales in his hand.
>
> Then I heard what sounded like a voice among the four living creatures saying, "A quart of wheat for a day's wages, and three quarts of barley for a day's

> wages, and do not damage the oil and the wine."
> Rev 6:5,6 (NIV)

In scripture, bread by weight always denotes famine and scarcity as does the colour black. This rider on the black horse accords with one of the major signs given in Matt 24; famine. For a days wages is worth only a small amount of wheat and barley which equates to a few slices of bread. There will be wide-spread famine in the Apocalypse and many will die as a result. When it says, '**do not damage the oil and the wine**', this could mean that the elites, who are ruling the world, will have control over the wine and oil and will not be affected by the famine. But receiving a little wheat and barley for a day's wages portends a world-wide economic and financial collapse. What we are witnessing at present is a very shaky financial situation which has never been experienced to such a wide extent by world economies before. This is just a foreshadow of what is to come which is represented by the rider on the black horse. That is, total economic collapse and widespread food shortages.

In ancient mythology, Mercury was knowm as the god of commerce, travel and thievery. Mercury is the Roman name who is associated with the Greek god Hermes, who acted as messenger between humans and the gods. His name in Latin is *Mercurius* from which we derive the words merchandise and merchant. It appears that this rider on the black horse is involved with commerce as depicted by the balances. So perhaps this rider on the famine horse is Mercury, who reigned alongside Apollo and Mars along with the other original pantheon of Olympian gods in the days of Noah. Could this demigod be the Minister for Finance in the coming rule of the New World Order, along with a human counterpart?

The rider on the pale horse is named as Death. Elsewhere in scripture the Angel of Death appears most noteably when the plagues struck Egypt prior to Moses leading the children of Israel across the Red Sea. Hades (the grave) follows after death just as pestilence follows famine. That Death and Hades are indeed angels is borne out by Rev 20:14 (KJV) which states:

> "And Death and Hell ( Hades) were cast into the lake of fire."

In 20:10 it tells us that, at the conclusion of the Millennial reign,

> '...the Devil that deceived them was cast into the lake of fire and brimstone, where the Beast and the False Prophet are...'

Just as these are fallen evil angels, so too the angel of Death and the god Hades will likewise be flung into the eternal lake of fire, which, Jesus told us, was **'reserved for the Devil and his angels'**. Hades in Greek mythology is the god of the nether regions or underworld and is associated with the Roman god, Pluto. Death rides on a pale horse hence the expression, as pale as death.

We noted earlier how that Satan always imitates and duplicates what the true God does. And in the very first chapter of the Book of Revelation, we have a description by John of Jesus Christ:

> " And I turned to see the voice that spake with me. And being turned I saw seven golden candlesticks; And in the midst of the seven candlesticks, one like unto the Son of Man...And He had in His right hand seven stars..."

Then in verse 20, Jesus explains what these represent:

> "The mystery of the seven stars which thou sawest in my right hand...The seven stars are the seven angels of the seven churches..." Rev 1:12,13,16 and 20 (KJV)

These seven angels are the seven spirits or angels who stand before the Throne of God. In Rev 8:2 it says:

" And I saw the seven angels which stood before God; and to them were given seven trumpets."

Thus, as seven angels stand before God, so too Satan has his seven angels, represented by the seven heads of the Beast, standing for him in opposition to the seven holy angels. It is interesting also that these same seven good angels are mentioned in relation to Jesus in chapter 5 and verse 6 of the same book:

> " And I beheld and lo, in the midst of the throne and of the four beasts, and in the midst of the elders, stood a Lamb, as it had been slain having seven horns and seven eyes, which are the seven Spirits of God sent forth into all the earth."

Again we note here that the Lamb, which is Jesus Christ, has seven horns which are seven angels and they are spirits. Contrast this with the beast from the Abyss which has seven heads which are also seven other spirits and fallen angels (besides the ten horns which are ten other fallen angels). How we marvel at how the Word will interpret itself for us if we will only go to it and it alone for enlightenment and understanding.

CHAPTER 10

# Apocalypse Soon

WHEN WE GO BEHIND the veil of the Apocalypse, we discover that it was a god of yore who was the king which led the other 200 Nephilim (according to the Book of Enoch),which fell to earth in those bygone days. These were the cause of the bloodshed and terror and violence which filled the world and brought on the Flood in the days of Noah. And for their sin, they have been locked up in Tartarus ever since awaiting the judgement of that great day.

It is this writer's opinion that these beings, when they re-appear on the world-stage, will be in full view as themselves to the public eye. That is, some believe that the Antichrist is a human who will be possessed by Satan. This view is contrary to what is revealed in scripture. But I believe that Apollo will be seen as himself, in person, as will the False Prophet and all the other gods who arise from Tartarus. For when these spirit men manifested themselves on the earth and mated with human women circa 5,500 years ago, it was they themselves in person who did these actions and not humans whom they possessed. "**As it was in the days of Noah...so shall it be.**"

Revelation chapter 11 next mentions the Antichrist and his interaction with the Two Witnesses. We briefly touched on this earlier but I would like to expand on some points here. These are two prophets of God who will preach on His behalf for three and a half years. In doing so, they will turn many to God and His Son, Jesus Christ.

> " And I will give power to my two witnesses...If anyone tries to harm them, fire comes from their mouths and devours their enemies.."
>
> These men have the power to shut up the sky so that it will not rain during the time they are prophesying; and they have the power to turn the waters into blood and to strike the earth with every kind of plague as often as they want." Rev 11:3,5,6 (NIV)

As was stated already, we are not given the names of these two witnesses. So we do not know who they are. But they have great power of God at their disposal and by this they win many souls over to God and His Son. As a result, they are a thorn in the side of the Antichrist and his minions.

> "Now when they have finished their testimony, the BEAST THAT COMES UP FROM THE ABYSS will attack them, and overpower and kill them..
>
> Their bodies will lie in the street of the great city which is figuratively called Sodom and Egypt, where also their Lord was crucified.
>
> For three and a half days men from every people, tribe, language and nation, will gaze on their bodies and refuse them burial. The inhabitants of the earth will gloat over them and will celebrate by sending each other gifts, because these two prophets had tormented those who live on the earth." Rev 11:7-10 (NIV)

If any normal man tries to interfere with the two witnesses, they are repelled. But the Beast from the Abyss is no ordinary man. He eventually attacks them and kills them. Their lifeless bodies will lie in the streets of Jerusalem for three and a half days. You will note that Jerusalem is called here, Sodom and Egypt, because when the Nephilim were on earth prior to the Flood and after it, they congregated to a large degree in both Sodom and its environs and in Egypt, where the relief's on the temple walls there depict these self-same gods. Global TV will cover the death of these prophets and all the people of the world will party at the death of God's two witnesses.

> "But after three and a half days, a breath of life from God entered them, and they stood on their feet, and terror struck those that saw them. Then they heard a loud voice from heaven saying, "Come up here". And they went up to heaven in a cloud while their enemies looked on." Rev 11:11,12 (NIV)

How the unbelievers of the world will be astonished as they watch their TV's and see the two men's lifeless bodies suddenly rise from the dead. I'm sure many a heart will fail and many a loin will be loosed when this prophecy comes to pass!

> "And that very hour there was a severe earthquake and a tenth of the city collapsed. Seven thousand people were killed in the earthquake and the survivors were terrified and gave glory to the God of heaven." Rev 11:13 (NIV)

Here again is another powerful prophecy that will serve to convince people that the Word of truth is a reality and will surely come to pass. For a massive earthquake will strike a section of Jerusalem after the two witnesses are caught up to heaven, and seven thousand people will perish. This event will serve to turn many a soul to the Most High God when it takes place, as surely it will. And the two witnesses being taken up from earth to heaven is a clear message to those Christians who profess that there is no Rapture mentioned in the Bible.

> "The second woe is passed. The third woe is coming." Rev 11:14 (NIV)

Chapters 13 and 17 provide the most information about the Antichrist .

> "And I saw a beast coming out of the sea. He had ten horns and seven heads, with ten crowns on his horns and on each head a blasphemous name...
>
> The dragon gave the beast his power and his throne and great authority. One of the heads of the beast seemed to have received a fatal wound, but the fatal wound had been healed." Rev 13:1-3 (NIV)

The ten horns are ten angels and they have crowns. The crowns represent the authority that they will receive when they receive their 'kingdoms'. That is, when the world is split into ten regions and each one will be in charge of a district, together with human politicians, under the supervision of the Beast who will be 'President of the World'.

The dragon, Satan, gives Christ/Apollo his throne and great authority. If the Antichrist is the head of a global UN, then it is because Satan puts him in place. Then the Antichrist receives a fatal head wound and is killed. Perhaps he will be assassinated. But he is then raised from the dead before the eyes of the whole world. The result is not a surprise. Rev 13:3,4 (NIV):

> "The whole world was astonished and followed the beast. Men worshipped the dragon because he had given authority to the beast, and they also worshipped the beast and asked, " Who is like the beast? Who can make war against him?"

The people of the world are in utter amazement. First they see this man killed in a violent way. Next thing he rises from the dead by the power of Satan in what is an obvious counterfeit resurrection. No wonder they believe this man to be the Messiah and that he, and only he, can solve all the problems facing the world and bring the peace that so many have longed for. There is an obvious hint in this last phrase that others are afraid to challenge the beast militarily. For they ask, 'Who can make war against him'? This implies that other powers are fearful of his military capacity and spiritual power and helps explain how he can force peace between nations. So they worship the Antichrist and they worship the Devil who had given such power to the Beast.

> "The beast was given a mouth to utter proud words and blasphemies and to exercise his authority for forty-two months. He opened his mouth to blaspheme God, and to slander his name and his dwelling-place and those who live in heaven.
>
> He was given power to make war against the saints and to conquer them. And he was given authority over every tribe, people language and nation." Rev 13:5-7 (NIV)

Notice here the Beast has authority over the whole world; **'every tribe, people, language and nation'**. His reign is not restricted just to the European Union, but to all of the globe.

This individual will have a foul mouth and will curse God and the Church of God and all those who dwell in heaven. He will then pursue those Christians who are trapped in this grim nightmare and many will lose their lives. It is of note here that the phrase used regarding the saints is that he will 'conquer them'. This is further proof that the Church of God in this present age of grace is not involved in this future time of Tribulation. For in Romans 8:37, which is specifically addressed to the born-again believers who are members of the Body of Christ, it says, **'we**

**are more than conquerors through him who loved us'**. Contrast this with those saints in the Apocalypse who will be 'the conquered'.

> "All inhabitants of the earth will worship the beast- all whose names have not been written in the book of life belonging to the Lamb that was slain from the foundation of the world.
>
> He who has an ear, let him hear. If anyone is to go into captivity, into captivity he will go. If anyone is to be killed with the sword, with the sword he will be killed.
>
> This calls for patient endurance and faithfulness on the part of the saints." Rev 13:8-10 (NIV)

This is another grave warning to those who presently sit on the fence and who have not accepted Jesus as their personal Lord and saviour. For the folks caught in this apocalyptic time-warp are to suffer ferocious torture and hardship and death and at hands of the Antichrist and his evil police forces. Later I will give my interpretation of the parable of the five wise and five unwise virgins which I believe is applicable to this study and these future times.

> "And I saw another beast coming out of the earth and he had two horns like a lamb, but he spake as a dragon. He exercised all the authority of the first beast on his behalf, and made the earth and its inhabitants worship the first beast, whose fatal wound had been healed.
>
> And he performed great and miraculous signs, even causing fire to come down from heaven to earth in full view of men. Because of the signs he was given the power to do on behalf of the first beast, he deceived the inhabitants of the earth." Rev 13:11-14 (NIV)

Here we have the rise of the False Prophet from his place of detention which is under the earth as opposed to under the sea. He has two horns who are kings, which means he is accompanied by two other fallen spirit men which makes three of them in total. The description of him as a lamb suggests he is of a religious nature. But he speaks like a dragon which means he is empowered of Satan who is the dragon.

As sidekick to the Antichrist, he exhibits signs, miracles and wonders on the Beast's behalf, whereby all the inhabitants of the world-whose name are not in the Lamb's book of life, are enthralled and deceived. It is the False Prophet who forces the peoples to worship the Antichrist who has been raised from the dead.

> "He ordered them to set up an image of the beast who was wounded by the sword and yet lived. He was given power to give breath to the image of the beast, so that it could speak and cause all who refused to worship the image to be killed." Rev 13:14,15 (NIV)

Now this is a spectacular occurrence and even more impressive than calling fire down from heaven in the sight of men. The False Prophet orders a statue of the Antichrist to be erected. This is not unusual as Nebuchadnezzar did the same thing in the days of Daniel, and all peoples were to bow down to his image in those days. The same applies with dictators today such as Saddam Hussein when he ruled Iraq and Chairman Mao in China. Statues of themselves could be seen everywhere and their pictures hung in every house. The present dictator of North Korea has statues of himself all over that country.

But the False Prophet goes a step further. When the image is erected, he will have the power to make the image come alive and speak. What a spectacle that will be. Now this is a trick that has never been seen before. No wonder all the people of the world will be at the whim of the Antichrist and ready to kill all those who oppose his word and who refuse to bow the knee to his image.

> "He also forced everyone, small and great, rich and poor, free and slave, to receive a mark on his right hand or on his forehead, so that no one could buy or sell unless he had the mark, which is the name of the beast or the number of his name.
>
> This calls for wisdom. If anyone has insight, let him calculate the number of the beast, for it is a man's number. His number is 666." Rev 13:16-18 (NIV)

One of my favourite writers on Biblical matters was an Englishman, EW Bullinger, who lived and wrote about 100 years ago. His *Commentary On Revelation* is a wonderful study which illustrates the great insight God gave to this humble scholar. Writing on the above verse, Bullinger says:

> "When the government of the Antichrist comes to power, there will be a system of accounting which will be able to keep track of the buying and selling of everybody in the entire world."

This is a remarkable statement when you consider it was written about 100 years ago when they had only begun using the telegraph. But in our day, this is a reality. For if I use my credit card to purchase an item in Los Angeles, the money is deducted from my account in Ireland some few seconds later.

So the technology exists today to literally keep track of the financial transactions of the whole population of the world. Most scholars agree that a microchip placed under the skin of the right hand or on the forehead is the mark of the Beast. Already RFID chips are being tested on families in the USA and Europe. And domestic and farm animals in the USA and elsewhere, have to have, by law, a microchip inserted with all their information encoded therein.

So the one-world government of the Antichrist will force everyone to have this mark and anyone who does not take it will be boycotted and unable to buy or sell or do business. So how will those who refuse to take the mark survive if they cannot buy the food and other goods they need in order to live day-to-day? This is another indication of how hard life will be for those Christians who realise what is going on at this time. They will need to forage for themselves and provide for their families as best they can.

So if you are reading this book and several hundred million born again Christian believers have vanished off the face of the earth, then you will know what is ahead and you will need to plant and sow and begin to make plans for how you and your family and fellow pilgrims are to survive the next few years. If you endure to the end, you will be rescued. But even if you do not survive and are to suffer and die at the hands of the Antichrist and the False Prophet, you must refuse the temptation to accept the mark of the Beast.

Choosing to accept the mark of the Beast and the number of his name is a decision that will have eternal consequences. This is not something that should be taken lightly. All those who are committed to the Antichrist and to his cause, will take the mark. Their names are not written in the book of life of the Lamb. But those people whose names are written in the book of life, they will not take this mark. An ominous warning is given to those who might consider acquiescing to the orders of the beast's one-world authorities.

> "If any man worship the beast and his image, and receive his mark in his forehead, or in his hand, ...he shall be tormented with fire and brimstone... and the smoke of their torment ascends up forever and ever; and they have no rest day nor night, who worship the beast and his image, and whosoever receives the mark of his name.
>
> Here is the patience of the saints: here are they that keep the commandments of God, and the faith of Jesus.

> And I heard a voice from heaven saying unto me, " Write: Blessed are the dead which die in the Lord from henceforth: Yea, saith the Spirit, that they may rest from their labours; and their works do follow them." Rev 14:9-13 (KJV)

Notice the contrast in the above sentiments. On the one hand we are given the grim truth regarding any who accepts the mark of the Beast. They receive eternal torment of fire and have no rest day or night forever. On the other hand, the saints of God are encouraged to have patience and to endure the hardship which will ensue as a result of refusing to accept the mark and of bowing the knee to the image of the Antichrist. When it says, **'Blessed are the dead which die in the Lord from henceforth'**, this is yet another insinuation as to the fierce testing that those Christians are to go through. But there is also encouragement here as those who endure will ultimately receive eternal salvation and see their saviour face-to-face. So the living hell and torture they will have to endure will be worth it and a reward will await them when finally this nightmare ends. I shall return to this theme in chapter 12.

As I write, the events of the Apocalypse are still future. The epistles of Paul addressed specifically to the Church of God all begin with the words, 'grace and mercy'. Grace means 'divine favour', and mercy is the withholding of merited judgement. It is by the grace and mercy of God that those of us who believe in Jesus Christ today are to be spared the nightmare of the coming wrath. How thankful we should be.

CHAPTER 11

# Babylon the Prostitute Exposed

CHAPTER 17 OF THE Book of Revelation provides us with the identity of the ten horns and seven heads and also introduces us to a great city that will be a feature of the End Times events. It names this city, '**Mystery: Babylon the Mother of Prostitutes and Abominations of the Earth**' and refers to her as '**a great whore who sits on many waters**'. John is told by one of the seven angels of God, that he will show him the judgement of the great whore and of the Beast that carries her. We will now examine some of the information in this chapter and see if we can make sense of the clues provided and speculate as to the possible identity of the great city it prophesies of. There are many cities throughout the world which fulfil some or all of the clues given here. And only when the Apocalypse arrives, and the Antichrist and his henchmen set up headquarters in this town, will we know for certain which city it is for sure.

In order to decode the clues that are provided in these two chapters regarding this 'great city', we have to do some lateral thinking. It is a bit like trying to figure out those puzzles that were in comic books when we were children. You remember those sketches of say, a farmhouse and barn with various farm implements scattered about the drawing. We were told there were ten chickens hidden in the picture and you had to find the ten. So you would notice a chicken sketched into and disguised in the wheel of the tractor. Then there would be another disguised in the chimney of the house. Then another in a haycock, and so one until you could find all ten. In the same way, the clues as to this future great city are hidden throughout chapters 17 and 18 of Revelation.

Speaking of the angel who spoke to John, it says:

> "So he carried me away in the Spirit into the wilderness : and I saw a woman sit upon a scarlet coloured beast, full of names of blasphemy, having seven heads and ten horns...And upon her forehead was a name written, MYSTERY; BABYLON THE GREAT, THE MOTHER OF HARLOTS AND ABOMINATIONS OF THE EARTH.
>
> And I saw the woman drunken with the blood of the saints and with the blood of the martyrs of Jesus: and when I saw her, I wondered with great admiration." Rev 17:3,5,6 (KJV)

Here we see that the harlot (whore or prostitute), which is a great city, sits on a scarlet coloured beast which has seven heads and ten horns. It says that this city is made drunk with the blood of the saints and martyrs of Jesus. Earlier in verse 2, we are told '**the inhabitants of the earth have been made drunk with the wine of her fornication**'. It would appear the 'wine' spoken of here is the same as the 'blood' of the Christians mentioned in verse 6, with whom the whore was made drunk. This seems to implicate the blood of the Christians with the city, Babylon; The Great, The Mother of Harlots. Put another way, the order to kill

Christians and spill their blood comes from those in power who reside in this great city.

This city sits on a beast which has ten horns and seven heads. We already know who these seven heads and ten horns are. But there is another point here which must be addressed. We will once again allow the Spirit to inform us so that we are in no doubt as to what is taking place. Here is the explanation:

> "And the angel said unto me, Wherefore didst thou marvel? I will tell thee the mystery of the woman, and of the beast that carries her, which hath the seven heads and ten horns...
>
> The seven heads are seven mountains on which the woman sits. They are also seven kings: five are fallen, one is and the other is not yet come: and when he cometh, he must continue a short space...And the ten horns which you saw are ten kings, which have received no kingdom as yet, but receive power as kings one hour with the beast." Rev 17:7,9,10,12 (KJV)

It tells us that the seven heads are seven mountains. Most commentators take this to mean that the city, known as Babylon the Great, sits on seven hills or mountains. They often assume that this is Rome as it sits on seven hills. They then construe that the whore is the Roman Catholic Church. But these same scholars omit to read the next phrase which says these seven mountains, **'are seven kings'** or rulers. When we arrive at the Book of Enoch, we will see that several times it speaks of seven burning mountains and defines them as being seven angels, and it describes the place where they will be banished to. So it refers to the seven angels metaphorically as seven mountains. Likewise the angel explains to John that the seven mountains on which the whore sits are seven kings and ten kings respectfully. That these rulers are fallen angels is obvious from the phrase, **'five have fallen, one is and one is to come'**.

Then in verse 15 we are provided with three more clues as to the identity of the woman:

> "And he saith unto me, The waters which thou sawest, where the whore sittest, are peoples, and multitudes and nations and tongues...And the woman which thou sawest is that great city, which reigneth over the kings of the earth." Rev 17:15,18 (KJV)

It plainly states here that, **'the woman you saw is that great city'**. Some commentators insist that Babylon the Great is a country or a city in the Near or Middle East while others assert it is the Roman Catholic Church. But no less than seven times it is termed a 'great city' here in Revelation chapters 17 and 18. For instance:

> "With such violence the great city of Babylon will be thrown down." Rev 18:21 (NIV)
> (See also Rev. 18:10,16,18,19)

So this great city is just that; a city. It is not a country or a Muslim empire or a religious denomination. Scripture repeatedly informs us that it is a great and powerful city. This city does two things here. It reigns over these kings or rulers who are 17 in total, and the waters it sits amongst represent a multitude from every nation and tongue and people and language. This clue means that the citizens of this city are multi-cultural and have arrived to live in this metropolis from the four corners of the globe. This city also **'reigns over the kings of the earth'**. What does this imply?

When the Antichrist assumes his power and high-office, the ten other kings will receive their geographic regions and power also. **'These have one mind, and shall give their power and strength unto the beast'** (verse 13). This means, they will be subject in authority unto the Antichrist and to his government. Again referring to the Beast, it says:

> "And the beast that was, and is not, even he is an eighth king, and is of the seven, and goeth into perdition." Rev 17:11 (KJV)

The implication seems to be that the Antichrist is associated with and one of the seven rulers and is also the supreme commander of the ten other rulers or kings who will in due course acquire their respective seats of power and regions to govern. Remember, 'king' is just another name for a ruler. And a ruler could be a President or a Prime Minister or a Governor or the head of an organisation. Now we have a clearer image emerging of this city. Just because it is called here, Babylon, this does not mean it is literally the Babylon of old which is situated in present day Iraq. For earlier in chapter 11, we have another city which is referred to as Sodom and Egypt, and then we are told that this city is, **'where also our Lord was crucified'**. Well we know that Jesus died in Jerusalem. So here we have two other evil locations, Sodom and Egypt, put as figures for the actual place, Jerusalem.

Likewise, Babylon is a figure pointing to a modern city which is great in power and influence in these last days. This city, we are informed, sits on or is made up of a multi-cultural population. We are told that this city 'reigns over the kings' or rulers who are to govern the ten geo-political regions during the Apocalypse. Another way of putting this is to say that the seat or headquarters of the government of the Antichrist from whence he will control his ten geo-political regions, will emanate from this great city. This is what is meant when it says:

> "And the woman which you saw is that great city, which reigns over the kings of the earth." Rev 17:18 (KJV)

In other words, the rulers of the earth will reign or govern *from this great city.*

Let us see what else Scripture has to say regarding this Whore of Babylon and how it might further clarify the real identity of this powerful town which will become the *de facto* capital of the world when these prophecies become reality. The whole of chapter 18 is given to foretelling the plight and end to this famous city. I will not quote every verse here, but will pluck out pertinent passages which may help elucidate our quest. The reader is advised to read this chapter carefully in order to gain a scope for what it is saying. Rev 18:2,3 (KJV):

> "And he (the angel) cried with a loud voice saying, "Babylon the great is fallen, is fallen, and is become the habitation of devils, and the hold of every foul spirit, and a cage of every unclean and hateful bird.
>
> For all nations have drunk of the wine of the wrath of her fornication, and the kings of the earth have committed fornication with her, and the merchants of the earth have waxed rich through the abundance of her delicacies."

This describes the fate of this great city. It is to fall. Rev 17:16 (KJV) tells us of its demise:

> "And the ten horns (rulers) which you saw upon the beast, these shall hate the whore (city), and shall make her desolate and naked, and shall eat her flesh, and burn her with fire."

Although the forthcoming rulers of the world take their orders from this great city, at some point in the future, they turn against it and **'burn her with fire'.** This truth is borne out several times in chapter 18. Speaking of this mighty metropolis it says:

> "Therefore shall her plagues come in one day, death and mourning, and famine; and she shall be utterly

> burned with fire: for strong is the Lord God who judges her.
>
> And the kings of the earth, who have committed fornication and lived deliciously with her, shall bewail her, and lament for her, when they shall see the smoke of her burning.
>
> Standing afar off for fear of her torment, saying, Alas, alas, that great city Babylon, that mighty city! For in one hour is thy judgement come.
>
> The merchants ... which were made rich by her, shall stand afar off for the fear of her torment, weeping and wailing...And cried when they saw the smoke of her burning, saying "What city is like unto this great city." Rev 18: 8,9,10,15,18 (KJV)

The downfall of this city will come suddenly, **'For in one hour is thy judgement come'**. And along with the burning judgement comes death and famine. Verse 21 (KJV) gives us a further mind-picture as to the fate of this important city:

> "And a mighty angel took up a stone like a great millstone, and cast it into the sea saying, "Thus with violence shall that great city Babylon be thrown down, and shall be found no more at all."

Because we are told four times here that this city will burn with fire, and because of the description of the angel casting a huge stone down into the sea, and all this is to happen in 'one hour', I believe this is describing a nuclear strike. Later in this book I will write of the final battle which will occur at the termination of the Apocalypse and is called Armageddon. It is a nuclear battle that will encompass the whole world which will result in the destruction of this and many other cities.

Here are some more clues from Revelation chapter 18 describing this mighty and dominant city. Because we are now in the

End Times, this municipality is now in existence and awaiting her role in the coming Apocalypse.

> " ...the merchants of the earth are waxed rich through the abundance of her delicacies...
>
> And the merchants of the earth shall weep and mourn over her; for no man buys their merchandise any more:
>
> The merchandise of gold, and silver and precious stones, and of pearls and fine linen, and purple, and silk, and scarlet, and all thymine wood, and all manner of vessels of ivory, and all manner vessels of most precious wood, and of brass, iron and marble.
>
> And cinnamon, and odours and ointments, and frankincense, and wine and oil and fine flour, and wheat and beasts, and sheep and horses, and chariots and slaves, and souls of men.
>
> The merchants of these things, which were made rich by her, shall stand afar off...saying, 'Alas, alas, that great city, that was clothed in fine linen, and purple and scarlet, and decked with gold, and precious stones and pearls.
>
> For in one hour so great riches is come to nought.' And every shipmaster, and all the company in ships, and sailors, and as many as trade by sea, stood afar off... And cried when they saw the smoke of her burning...
>
> ...Saying, "alas, alas, that great city, wherein were made rich all that had ships in the sea by reason of her costliness, for in one hour is she made desolate."
>
> Rev 18:3, 11-13, 15-19 (KJV)

What is immediately apparent here is that this city is a major sea-trading port. Every product imaginable is traded in this city. Even slaves and the souls of men are available in this mighty city which is not so far-fetched as sex slavery is common across the world today. All the rich merchants will weep when they see this city burning for nobody will buy their goods anymore. Several times it mentions how businessmen were made rich by trading with her; '**Merchants of the earth grew rich by the abundance of her delicacies'** and, **'Your merchants were the worlds great men'**. Brokers, traders, importers, exporters and entrepreneurs, all became fabulously rich through dealing in this city.

Jeremiah the prophet also speaks of this great city when he prophesies of Babylon in chapters 50-51 of that book. There are obvious parallel prophecies here referring to this same city and to the country as a whole. We know these prophecies are pertaining to the Last Days because of the expression used several times there:

> "Since this is the vengeance of the Lord."
> Jer 50:15 (NIV)
> "It is the time of the Lord's vengeance."
> Jer 51:6 (NIV)

This is the Day of Vengeance that we discussed at the start of this book when Jesus closed the scroll before reading this phrase. There are no less than 13 similar references in these two chapters clearly showing that these predictions refer to this city and the time of the Apocalypse. Hear this clue in 51:53 (NIV):

> "Even if Babylon reaches the sky and fortifies her lofty strongholds, I will send destroyers against her, declares the Lord."

And Jer 50:15 (NIV):

> "She surrenders, her towers fall, her walls are torn down. Since this is the vengeance of the Lord."

This city reaches to the sky, has lofty strongholds and her towers will fall. The 'destroyers' refer to the fallen angels who work on behalf of the Destroyer who will burn her with fire at the close of the Apocalypse when this powerful metropolis is obliterated along with the rest of the cities in her country. We know this is the fate of this country because in this same prophesy Jeremiah foretells:

> "This is the Word of the Lord spoken through Jeremiah the prophet concerning Babylon and the land of the Babylonians." Jer 50:1 (NIV)

And:

> "Before your eyes I will repay Babylon and all who live in Babylonia." Jer 51:24 (NIV)

This shows that not only will the city be destroyed but also the whole country. Many cities throughout the world might qualify based on these clues. London is a major financial centre and is by the sea. In the Far East, Singapore is a major financial trading centre as is Tokyo in the economically influential Japan. China has emerged recently as one of the richest and most powerful empires in world economic terms. Hong Kong is its financial centre and, like Singapore and Tokyo, has huge skyscrapers and towers and are situated by the sea having great harbours.

There are many other prophecies in Jeremiah chapters 50 and 51 which mirror those provided in Revelation 17 and 18.

Let us summarise all the hints decoded thus far:

- The implication is that this great city is a sea trading city.
- Everything is for sale that anyone could ever want to buy in this city.
- It is the financial centre for world trade and commerce.
- Businessmen have made vast fortunes by trading with this city.
- This city has high towers that reach to the sky.
- This city has a multi-cultural population drawn from all corners of the globe.
- The headquarters of the government of the Antichrist will rule from its offices in this wealthy city.

- This city is described as 'the Mother of Prostitutes' and has a golden cup in her hand.
- This city is also an evil city as all manner of sin and godlessness will operate there.

Now let us speculate as to what all this means by comparing this future set-up with what exists in the political framework and power structures of today. The world organisation which has much worldly power and influence at present is the United Nations or UN. It has a head and several permanent members. Its headquarters are in New York which has a population of people from every quarter of the world. That is, it is multi-cultural and I recently read that 35% of the population of New York are non American and from outside the USA. The rest of the citizens are of multi-ethnic origin. However it must be said that much of the populations of many of the great cities of the world today are multicultural. It seems to be a policy of world leaders these days to break down borders and allow citizens from different countries travel and live in any country they choose. Thus in London, for instance, the inhabitants and mix of races is phenomenal. The same can be said of Paris and France which now has five million Muslims living in that country.

Wall Street in New York is the centre of all the world's financial and commercial trading. Businessmen and financial brokers have made massive fortunes via Wall Street. New York has a sea port which attracts cargoes from everywhere. Therefore it must figure as a possible contender to be the city that is called in prophecy, Babylon. The UN could be the organisation by which the Antichrist will exercise his power. For when one listens to the leaders of the New World Order when they speak of their grand plans to have a one-world government, they always speak of the UN as the vehicle whereby they will achieve these goals.

The 'seven heads' could be the G-7 or the seven permanent members who sit in the United Nations headquarters which are in New York. And the ten other rulers are those ten who will be the Prime Ministers or Premiers who govern their regions under the ultimate power of their leader, the President or head of the UN, otherwise known as the Antichrist or the Beast from the Bottomless Pit. Having said that, the UN and other clandestine organisations who have as their members world leaders, often meet in different countries and different continents.

Many authors insist that Babylon in Iraq is to be re-built and will be the centre of power in the future. To me, this is a non-sense. Present day Babylon is a mere shadow of its former glory of thousands of years ago when it ruled the world. Although Saddam Hussein re-built a few of its buildings, it is a mere ruin today, wasting away in the desert. Its closest sea port is hundreds of miles away and it is not the centre of world trade and of the riches described in Revelation 18. Neither is present day Babylon multi-cultural in its population. It is populated mostly by one tribe; Arab. In the list of great cities of today, Babylon does not even register. Nor is there any chance that it will emerge any time soon as a player on the world-stage.

The last verse in this chapter of Rev 18:24 is a haunting one:

> "And in her (the city) was found the blood of prophets and of saints, and of all that were slain upon the earth."

This suggests that the orders to hunt down and kill Christians will come from the powers-that-be who hold their high office in this city. And not just the blood of Christians, but **'of all that were slain upon the earth'**. This figure will run into billions by the end of the Great Tribulation period. We know this because John was given the figures when he received the revelation of what is to happen in the Last Days.

In observing world events that are occurring presently, it is obvious that the foundations of a one-world government are now being laid. Daily we hear politicians from differing countries telling us we need a New World Order and global cooperation between political powers in order to tackle the economic and environmental problems the world now faces. The United Nations is being touted as the vehicle whereby this governance is achieved. Meetings between global leaders are routinely held to forge relations and find a new way forward. Indeed, some might say that these plans by our leaders are positive and beneficial to mankind and to ensuring our survival into the future. But to the spiritually minded, we can see that all these grand plans are a foreshadowing of the coming Apocalypse and of the man of sin who will assume power and control of the New World Order which will end in the destruction of almost the whole world.

> "And I heard another voice from heaven saying,
> "Come out of her my people, that ye be not partakers
> of her sins, and that ye receive not of her plagues."
> Rev 18:4 (KJV)

Jeremiah the prophet echoes this. Chapter 51:45 (NIV) states; **'Come out of her my people! Run for your lives'**. And in verse 42 is an almost unbelievable prophecy concerning this future 'great city'.

> "The sea will rise over Babylon; its roaring waves
> will cover her."

When I contemplated this truth, I thought it too far-fetched to be considered. But as you will see in a later chapter, when Armageddon occurs, there will be a world-wide nuclear conflagration. Imagine the seismic effect on the earth's crust of perhaps 40,000 nuclear warheads all exploding about the same time? This would result in massive waves racing across the oceans of the world in all directions. Thus, **'its roaring waves will cover her'**. This city will be submerged by a mega Tsunami.

If you are in the time of Tribulation and are a resident of the city which is the headquarters of the Antichrist, this warning could not be more clear. You have got to leave or else be caught up in the judgement that will befall this immoral metropolis.

Also notice that it says of this city that it has become **'the habitation of devils and every foul spirit and a cage for every hateful bird'**(Rev 18:2 KJV). This is referring to the fallen angels. For the Devil and his evil spirit angels will be cast down to earth about the same time that Apollo and his foul spirits ascend from the Bottomless Pit (more on this in chapter 15). This is why this city is figuratively referred to as Babylon, and Jerusalem is called Sodom and Egypt. For Babylon and Sodom and Egypt were the habitation of these filthy spirit men when they first resided on this earth both before and after the Flood of Noah. Thus, during the Apocalypse both Jerusalem and this influential city will be infested by these beings.

It is interesting to note the role Hollywood is playing in preparing and conditioning the world for the manifestation of these fallen ones. For a huge amount of movies and TV programmes all feature aliens or ET's or angels or UFO's coming from space to earth and interacting with mankind. Feature films and television programmes and books have been pushing this agenda for several decades now. UFO sightings and abductions and alien encounters are an almost daily occurrence. This, I believe, is to soften the ground and make ready the world for the manifestation of the fallen angels, most of whom will descend from above and fall to earth like figs falling from a fig tree, shaken by a mighty wind, after they are ejected from heaven (Revelation chapters 6 and 12).

CHAPTER 12

# THE COMING SLAUGHTER OF CHRISTIANS

IN THE MIDST OF chapters 17 and 18, which tell of the coming Beast with seven heads and ten horns, and of the city that will reign over these rulers, is a verse that seems out of context. For in 17:14 this message is dropped in in the middle of all the prophecies regarding the Antichrist and the ten other kings and seven fallen angels. Speaking of the plight of the fallen angels it says:

> "These shall make war with the Lamb and the Lamb shall overcome them: for He is Lord of lords and King of kings: and they that are with Him are called and chosen and faithful."

Of course this is referring to the last battle which will occur at the end of the Great Tribulation and begin in the Valley of Meggido in Northern Israel. But the words that caught my eye here are those which mention who will accompany the King of kings when he defeats the hordes of Satan at Armageddon. It tells us that the people who will be with Jesus when He returns are the, **'called, the chosen and the faithful'**. This is not a description of angels. But it does describe believers. This reinforces the right doctrine that when Jesus returns to earth at the end of the Apocalypse, His called out and chosen people will be with Him. This is the Church of God or Body of Christ. That is, those born again believers who accepted Jesus as their personal Lord and Saviour before the events of the Book of Revelation begin. For how can His chosen and called out and faithful ones be with Him when He returns if we are already on earth and going through the Tribulation? We cannot. For He has already taken out His Church and brought them to His Father's house, just as He promised in John 14:1-4. When it describes the gathering together of the saints in 1 Thessalonians 4, it concludes (verse 17), **'And so shall we ever be with the Lord'**. So it makes perfect sense that when Jesus returns to defeat the archenemy at the conclusion of the Apocalypse, his called and chosen saints will accompany him.

Perhaps this is a good time to discuss the parable of the ten virgins, as it has come to be known. This is a story which has baffled people. But when we examine it in the light of Revelation, I believe we can literally understand its meaning. I shall proceed by quoting the parable verbatim.

> "Then shall the kingdom of heaven be likened unto ten virgins which took their lamps and went forth to meet the bridegroom. And five of them were wise and five were foolish.
>
> They that were foolish took their lamps and took no oil with them. But the wise took oil in their vessels with their lamps.
>
> While the bridegroom tarried, they all slumbered and slept. And at midnight there was a cry made; "Behold, the bridegroom cometh; go ye out to meet him."
>
> Then all those virgins rose and trimmed their lamps. And the foolish said unto the wise, "Give us of your oil; for our lamps are gone out."

But the wise answered, saying, "Not so, lest there be not enough for us and you: but go ye rather to them that sell, and buy for yourselves."

And while they went to buy, the bridegroom came; and they that were ready went in with him to the marriage and the door was shut.

Afterward came also the other virgins, saying; "Lord. Lord, open to us."

But he answered and said, "Verily I say unto you, I know you not."

Watch therefore, for ye know neither the day nor the hour wherein the Son of man cometh."

Matt 25:1-13 (KJV)

Let us take the last statement first. We don't know the day nor the hour that the Son of man cometh. So Jesus is talking here about His coming. Thus He is the bridegroom. When the call is made that His arrival was imminent, the five wise virgins were to, **'go ye out to meet him'**. These went with the bridegroom to the marriage feast and the door was shut. When the unwise virgins had returned, it was too late. They had missed the boat. The horse had already bolted. The train had left the station.

To my mind there is only one explanation as to what Jesus was teaching in this parable. He was talking about what Paul calls the 'gathering together' of the saints and our blessed hope. Many evangelicals call this, the Rapture. It is clearly stated in 1 Thessalonians 4, that the Lord is to return briefly and take out or catch away those that have believed in Him. First, the dead Christians since Pentecost are to rise and receive a new spiritual body (like the body Jesus received when He rose from the dead), and meet the Lord in the air. Then, those Christians who are alive will be caught up to meet the Lord also in the air. And so shall we ever be with the Lord.

He then takes His bride to the place He has been preparing for them since His ascension into heaven. He promised in John 14: 1-4, that He was going to His Father's house to prepare a place for His followers. He added that He would return and bring them to this place at a future date. So the parable of the 10 virgins is an explanation of what is to happen when He returns to fulfil this vow. Jesus will return in the air and His bride will go out to meet Him. These are those Christians who have accepted Him as their personal Lord and saviour and believe God raised him from the dead (Romans 10:9). They have their lamps trimmed and are ready.

On the other hand, we have the unwise virgins who are not ready. By the time they realise what is happening, it is too late and they are left behind. These are those who will turn to Jesus after the gathering together, when they comprehend what has occurred. Let me explain how this will happen. If we take the USA as an example, it has roughly 300 million population. Barna Research suggests that around 35% would proclaim that they are born-again. Obviously this leaves 65% who are not Christians.

However, many of these have heard of Jesus Christ and His salvation message. They know about the Rapture, but they choose to ignore it. They are well aware of much of the teachings of Jesus because they hear these day in, day out on radio and on TV. Many celebrities who are Christians have spoken about their faith and of the imminent Rapture and of the need to be ready. But these warnings are ignored. So what will happen?

Picture this; you wake up one morning and turn on the news and hear a most disturbing bulletin-millions of people from every corner of the world have mysteriously vanished. You find it hard to believe, but as news from around the world filters through and confirms this mass disappearance, a shiver of foreboding and trepidation runs through your body. You feel vulnerable, unsure and perhaps alone. The realisation that the Rapture has happened hits you like a baseball bat. You feel nauseous as the blood drains from your face and a dread fear creeps into the pit of your stomach. A fear you know is going to remain for some years to come. You are left on earth and you know that the prophecies have come to pass and now you must face into the woeful times talked about in the Apocalypse, along with all those others who refused to heed the warnings. You are part of those left behind. You drop to your knees and beg God and Jesus to forgive you and help you. The dark night of the soul has begun.

Huge amounts of people are going to become Christian believers after the Great Tribulation begins. These are the unwise virgins of the parable. These Christians will go through an horrific experience for the next several years. Some scholars say the Apocalypse is to last seven years. Others say three and a half. Either way it is going to be a literal hell on earth for all who find themselves ensnared in this demonic coliseum. Many verses in Revelation hint at the terror which is to befall these beleaguered Christians. Revelation refers often to the followers of Christ and calls them saints. This word in Greek means 'set apart' and is used throughout the Epistles when speaking of Christian believers.

> " Another angel, who had a golden censer, came and stood at the alter. He was given much incense to offer, with the prayers of all the saints, on the golden alter before the throne.
>
> The smoke of the incense, together with the prayers of all the saints, went up before God from the angel's hand."
>
> "The four living creatures and the twenty four elders fell down before the Lamb. Each one had a harp and they were holding golden bowls full of incense which are the prayers of the saints." Rev 8:3,4 and Rev 5:8 (NIV)

My sense from this is that there will be a lot of prayers emanating from the followers of Jesus during the time of Tribulation. This is quite understandable when we look at the activities of the Beast and of the False Prophet who will hunt them down. Speaking of the Beast it tells us:

> "He was given power to make war against the saints and to conquer them...He who has an ear, let him hear. If anyone is to go into captivity, into captivity he will go. If any is to be killed with the sword, with the sword he will be killed." Rev 13:7,9,10 (NIV)

> "I saw the woman was drunk with the blood of the saints, the blood of those who bore testimony to Jesus." Rev 17:6 (NIV)

> "In her (Babylon) was found the blood of the prophets and of the saints." Rev 18:24 (NIV)

Christian believers are to be killed and imprisoned because of their faith during this time. This would be no surprise as the 'god of this world' knows the prophecies and is preparing for them. Whole families will suffer extreme persecution and agony and hardship. It is going to be an horrific period.

This sentiment is further enhanced in chapter 14 which tells of the torment that those who take the mark of the Beast will go through for eternity. We covered this already, but there is no rest for those who worship the Beast or who take his mark. They will be tormented with burning sulphur forever and ever. It is obvious that many professing Christians may be tempted to accept this mark in order to do business and live and provide for their family. For right after this warning we are given an admonition:

> "This calls for patient endurance on the part of the saints who obey God's commandments and remain faithful to Jesus.

> Then I heard a voice saying, "Blessed are the dead who die in the Lord from now on."
> "Yes" says the Spirit, "they will rest from their labour, for their deeds will follow them." Rev 14:12,13 (NIV)

Prophecies in the Book of Daniel 11:33-35 (NIV) mirror these sentiments.

> "Those who are wise will instruct many though for a time they will fall by the sword or be burned or captured or plundered.
> When they fall, they will receive little help and many who are not sincere will join them. Some of the wise shall stumble, so that they may be refined, purified and made spotless until the time of the end, for it will still come at the appointed time."

And in Daniel 12:10 (NIV) we are told:

> "Many will be purified, made spotless and refined, but the wicked will continue to be wicked. None of the wicked will understand: but those who are wise will understand."

Not only will Christians be put to the sword, they will also suffer death by burning. In chapter 13 of the Book of Isaiah we have further prophecies concerning those who put their faith in God and Jesus during the Day of Tribulation. We know this is speaking of the time of the Apocalypse because Isaiah states several times that this passage concerns the 'day of Wrath' and the 'day of the Lord'(Isaiah 13:3,6). This is a harrowing prophecy but mature Christians need to hear this so that we can warn others as to what is coming down the tracks in the days ahead:

> "Like a hunted gazelle, like sheep without a shepherd...each will flee to his native land...Whosoever is captured will be thrust through; all who are caught

> will fall by the sword. Their infants will be dashed to pieces before their eyes; their houses will be looted and their wives ravished... Their bows will strike down the young men; they will have no mercy on infants nor will they look with compassion on children" Isaiah 13:14-16,18 (NIV)

The overriding message for those Christians in this time is, faithfulness to God and Jesus, and patient endurance. One can only guess at the horrors which will befall whole families and communities in this terrible holocaust. They will be hunted down, thrown in jail, tortured, beheaded and slaughtered in great numbers by the Antichrist and those who follow his orders, whose names are not in the Book of Life of the Lamb. But instead they are wedded to the worship of the Antichrist and his one-world system.

I have often received correspondence from fellow Christians insisting that we are indeed to go through the Great Tribulation and I am but a coward for not wanting to accept this trial of faith. On pointing out that we are 'saved from the coming wrath', I was informed, and this is a direct quote here, that "the true disciple of Jesus will be spared and protected from evil during this terrible time". But the passages quoted above relate to **'those who obey God's commandments and remain faithful to Jesus'**, and **'those who bore testimony to Jesus'**. These are not wishy-washy believers here. So those who teach that the Church, the *ecclesia* of God, are to suffer the wrath, are plainly in error and have not bothered to rightly divide the Word of God.

Thus we can see the meaning of the parable of the ten virgins. Those who accept Jesus as Lord in this present time, will be gathered together when the Lord returns before the events of the Apocalypse begin and before the Antichrist is released from his prison in the pit of the Abyss. Those who realise they are stuck in the web of the Great Tribulation are the unwise virgins who were not ready for his coming. They must now endure the savage testing that is to be their wont in the ensuing years of tyranny under the power of the Antichrist's global army. May God bless those who have to endure this period. If any are reading this before the Rapture and have not yet come to know the Lord Jesus, now is your chance to pull back from the brink of the dark Abyss into which the world will soon be plunged. Accept the free gift of eternal life made available to you by the finished work of the shedding of the blood of Jesus Christ. All you have to do is believe and ask, and it shall be given.

> " And you shall know the truth, and the truth shall set you free." Jesus Christ John 8:32 (KJV)

Many authors and commentators and Bible teachers say that the Parable of the Ten Virgins has nothing to do with the Rapture and the Church of God. I decided to dig a little deeper into this parable and see if the Word can clear up any confusion regarding its interpretation. So let us go through the story as presented line-by-line with the help of a Greek scholar whom I have consulted and, by the grace of God, may we come to a better understanding of its true meaning. Matthew 25:1

> "Then shall the kingdom of heaven be likened unto ten virgins which took their lamps and went forth to meet the bridegroom."

So the context set here is ten virgins going out to meet their bridegroom. This parable is the middle one of three which are all dealing with the same subject i.e. **"Watch therefore for ye know not what hour your Lord doth come."** (Matt 24:42) The first parable is known as the parable of the faithful and wise servant. Then we have the ten virgins and thirdly, the parable of the talents. All three are concerned with the same theme; namely, the going away and coming back of the Lord. And all three encourage us to; **"Therefore be ye ready; for in such an hour as ye think not, the Son of man cometh."**

Of course the whole of Matthew 24 and 25 are a response to a question to Jesus by some of his closest confidants as to what would be the signs of His second coming (*parousia*), and of the end of this age. So the three parables are a sort of summing up of what he had told them regarding the signs of the coming Apocalypse, what would happen during the Apocalypse, and what would occur after the Tribulation. All these are covered in Matt 24 and 25.

So the context of the Ten Virgins parable is the coming of the Lord and their going out to meet him.

> "And five of them were wise and five were foolish. They that were foolish took their lamps and took no oil with them. But the wise took oil in their vessels with their lamps. While the bridegroom tarried, they all slumbered and slept."

Many teachers have proposed that the word 'virgins' should be translated as 'bridesmaids'. Thus, they conclude that the marriage has already happened, the Bride (Church) is already in heaven and therefore these five wise bridesmaids represent those saints who are to go through the Tribulation and they will meet their Lord when he comes back at the end of the Apocalypse. In order to test this thesis, I wrote to an aged scholar who lives near Athens, Greece, and with whom I have become friendly over the past few years. Manos Nomikos has written several books and has translated others from Greek to English and vice versa. He is also a committed Christian. I told him what was being proposed by several writers in the USA who say these five are bridesmaids and asked him about the Greek word *parthenos* which is the word in the text for 'virgin'. Here is his reply verbatim:

> "Regarding the Ten Virgins, I can assure you that in Greek, both ancient and modern, any female that has

> not come into sexual intercourse with a male, and has not lost her maiden membrane, is a *parthenos*, i.e. "virgin", irrespective of what some scholars claim. It is noticeable that the Zodiac sign of Virgin in Greek is called *Parthenos*."

It is quite clear from this that 'virgins' is the proper and true rendering of the Greek text. Therefore to suggest that these virgins are actually bridesmaids is to make the Word say something other than its true meaning which is not in the original text.

In fact the word for 'bride' in Greek is *nymphe,* and the Greek for 'bridesmaids' is *paranymphos.* Neither of these words are found anywhere in the Gospels or epistles referring to the Church or to the bridegroom. You have to go to Revelation 21 to find the word 'bride' and this is a description of the New Jerusalem descending out of heaven. So to suggest that these five are not virgins and to say they are bridesmaids totally changes the meaning of the parable and skews it to allow a different interpretation be put on the story.

For if these virgins are changed to bridesmaids, this suggests that the bride is a different entity and it is a small step to suppose that she is already in heaven and the Marriage Feast with the groom is long over and done with. This is a presumption and is not the case. We read on.

> "And at midnight there was a cry made, 'Behold the bridegroom cometh; go ye out to meet him'. Then all those virgins arose and trimmed their lamps. And the foolish said unto the wise; 'Give us of your oil, for our lamps are gone out'.
>
> But the wise answered and said, 'Not so, lest there be not enough for us and you. But go ye rather to them that sell and buy for yourselves."

Most scholars agree that the oil is representative of the Holy Spirit. So the wise virgins represent those that have received the

Holy Spirit. Again this concurs with the Church Epistles that tell us that when we believed in the Lord we received the seed of God which is the gift of Holy Spirit. As a result we are the **'sons of God...in the midst of a crooked and perverse nation, among whom ye shine as lights in this world'**. It is interesting to note also that the virgins were directed to 'go ye out to meet him'. For this is what will occur when the Rapture takes place. We are going out to meet the Lord in the air. On the other hand, when Jesus returns with his Church at Armageddon, the Tribulation saints are not going out to meet him. Rather he is returning to earth to them.

> "And when they went to buy, the bridegroom came; and they that were ready went in with him to the marriage and the door was shut.
>
> Afterward also came the other virgins saying, 'lord, lord, open to us'. But he answered and said, 'Verily I say unto you, I know you not."

Now there are a couple of important points at issue here. Firstly, when the bridegroom came, the five wise virgins were ready to go and meet him and together they went to the marriage and the door was shut. As far as I am aware, there is only one marriage feast between the Lord and His church. This occurs in heaven after the Rapture and while the Apocalypse is happening on earth. So if the Bride is already in heaven, as some propose, then what marriage is this referring to?

In Matthew 22:1-14 there is another parable speaking about the same marriage. The marriage is prepared by the king for his son but all those that are invited refuse to come. So the king sends his servants into the highways and byways and invites as many as they can find to come to the marriage feast. You know the story. The invited guests were the Jews. But they would not come. The people who did come represent the Gentiles who are the Church.

But the point is, it is speaking of the same marriage between the son of the king and his chosen. So when the wise virgins meet their groom and go into the marriage feast and the door is shut, this has to be a reference to the Marriage Feast in heaven that we will all be attending someday soon. It cannot be that the marriage took place seven years earlier and the Bride is already in heaven and now there is a second marriage.

Here is another point; when the five unwise virgins return, they knock on the door and ask to be allowed in. Of course it is too late. But the clear inference here is that when they returned, they had oil in their lamps. They went off to buy oil, and returned with it. This suits the thesis which suggests these unwise virgins represent those masses of people who will turn to God and Jesus after the Rapture and during the Tribulation. Sure they will receive the Holy Spirit (oil) and bare testimony to Jesus. But it will be too late to get them to the marriage feast as the Rapture will have already passed. The unwise virgins likewise cannot represent unbelievers during the Tribulation. For they hate Jesus and have no interest in trying to gain entry to the marriage and will not be banging on the door shouting, 'lord, lord, let us in'.

Some say that this whole section has to do with the Jews and has nothing to do with the Church of the Body. I agree. But often there are dual or more meanings to prophetic statements. Thus even though Jesus is addressing the 'lost tribe of Israel' here, he is also speaking of the church to come post Pentecost and the gathering together of the saints. Others suggest that Jesus never spoke of the Rapture because this was only revealed to Paul later on. I disagree. Jesus plainly speaks of the Rapture in John 14:1-4 and also right here in Matt 24:40, 41(KJV):

> "Then shall two be in the field; the one shall be taken and the other left. Two women shall be grinding at the mill; the one shall be taken and the other left."

I know that many people will say that this not referring to the Rapture. They say for instance, 'one shall be taken for judgement, and the other left to go through the Tribulation', or some such argument. But hold on a minute; did we not just learn that you cannot change words to make them say something that is not written? You cannot change 'virgin' to 'bridesmaids' in order to suit your own theory as to what this parable means. To do so is to play fast and loose with the Word of God.

Remember the lesson from Genesis 3 when the Devil deceived Adam and Eve? God had given specific instructions to them regarding the tree of the knowledge of good and evil. Then along came Old Nick and started to debate with them. First he questioned what God had said; then he omitted a word; then he added to what was said, then he changed a word, and finally, he flat out contradicted what the Word said. The pattern is usually the same when it comes to interpreting Scripture. The point being, you cannot go around adding to or subtracting from what the plain truth states in order to suit a particular interpretation. And in the above quote, if it says, '**then shall two be in the field, one shall be taken and the other left**', then that's what it means. Leave it at that and accept it. **'Two women will be grinding. One shall be taken and the other left'**. That is what it says and that is what it means. It does not need us to add on a few more words. That's what Satan did in the garden. I have no doubt this is referring to the Rapture because the context of Matt 24 and 25 is in answer to the question, 'what is going to happen when you return'? Remember, these are the words of Jesus Christ who was no ordinary mortal prophet.

As I said, there is no mention anywhere in the Gospels or epistles of the Church being the Bride of Christ. However, it does refer to believers as 'virgin'. 2 Corinthians 11:2 (KJV):

"For, I am jealous over you with a godly jealousy; for I have espoused you to one husband that I may present you as a chaste virgin to Christ."

So there you have it. The epistle to the Corinthians is addressed to the Church of the Body of Christ. This compares the believers to a chaste virgin and ties them in with the five wise virgins (not bridesmaids), who went out to meet their bridegroom who took them to the marriage feast and shut the door behind them.

Although the Church is never called the Bride of Christ, it is actually inferred in Ephesians 5:22-33 where it likens the relationship of a wife and husband to that of Christ and His church. Paul finishes with, **"This is a great mystery: but I speak concerning Christ and the church"**.

But what is *not* a mystery is that the five wise virgins represent the church and when we go out to meet Him in the Rapture, then the door will be shut and those poor souls who will believe in Christ afterwards, will be left to suffer the horrible events which will soon fall upon the earth.

In the meantime, we are to **'watch therefore, for you know not what hour your Lord cometh'**. This is referring to the church today. For, we do not know when Jesus will return to gather us together in the air. It might happen tonight or it may happen in 50 years time. But the Tribulation saints, on the other hand, they *will* know when Jesus is coming back. They will know that he is coming at the end of the Apocalypse when the armies are gathered at the Valley of Megiddo and the Beast from the Abyss, the Antichrist, goes into the Temple declaring that he is God. So they will have a fair idea of exactly when Jesus is returning to earth whereas we today have no inkling as to when the Rapture will occur. Sure we have a hope that it will be soon as we can see the signs being fulfilled all around us. But we just do not know. It may be some time yet.

I do not mean to discredit those teachers and people who hold to a different interpretation of the Parable of the Ten Virgins. We are all brothers and sisters in Christ and we all want to do the right thing and rightly divide the Word of truth. But we are also encouraged to be like those Berean believers who searched the scriptures daily, whether those things were true. Many great scholars such as EW Bullinger, Hal Lindsey, Dave Hunt and Charles Capps amongst others agree that the five wise virgins represent the Church.

CHAPTER 13

# Enoch, the Watchers and the Occult

THE BOOK OF ENOCH has much to say regarding the fallen angels which it terms, 'the Watchers'.

Enoch was the seventh from Adam and was born circa 3382BC. There are only a few verses that mention Enoch which conclude in Genesis 5:22 which tell us that, **'Enoch walked with God: and was not: for God took him'**. This implies that Enoch did not die but was taken to heaven where he was shown visions of the future. Enoch 'walked with God'. This is the highest compliment that could be made to an Old Testament prophet as there are only a few men in the whole of the Bible where it says, they 'walked with God', yet it tells us this twice in the four verses that mention his name. This is another indication of the high regard God had for Enoch and that we should take notice of the writings of this exalted individual.

The Book of Enoch is not currently regarded as part of the canon of scripture. However, the ancient scholars were well versed in the Book of Enoch. It was obviously well known to Jesus and His disciples, for as we already stated, His brother, Jude, quotes directly from Enoch in his epistle.

> "And Enoch also, the seventh from Adam, prophesied of these, saying, behold, the Lord cometh with ten thousands of his saints." Jude 14 (KJV)

There are over 70 phrases in the Book of Enoch which directly relate to phrases in the New Testament. Much of his writings also relate to prophecies that are to occur in the time of the Apocalypse. Enoch also provides vivid descriptions of a dread place deep in the earth where fallen angels are imprisoned which sounds like the bottomless pit we have been reading about.

I will be quoting from *The Book of Enoch* by Ronald K. Brown, GBTS Press, San Antonio, Texas. This is an excellent book with notes and references that will be an addition to anyone wanting to study this important work. In the preface to his book, Ronald Brown states:

> "This work is not an apologetic to those who would refute the authenticity of the work of Enoch the Prophet, but it is an effort to further spread the Gospel of Jesus Christ. And like all other works by the ecclesia, it will likewise find opposition from the adversary. Some would claim that if this book were credible it would have been included in our Bibles today. But those making this argument are probably not aware that it was in the Bible for over 500 years.
>
> If placed back in the Bible, the Book of Enoch would further strengthen and revolutionize many theological axioms on angels, demons, final judgement, of creation etc., and validate statements made by writers of Old and New Testament scripture.
>
> The Book of Enoch gives illumination to the origin of many statements made by many Old Testament prophets such as Moses in Gen 6:2-4, Peter in 2 Peter 2:2, Paul in 2 Corinthians 12:2 and by Jesus in Mat-

thew 25:41 and many other passages of scripture in the Old and New Testaments of our Bible."

With this in mind, we quote from sections of the Book of Enoch. This is chapter 21 and depicts a place for incarcerated angels. Note the descriptions of 'seven stars' which are seven angels.

"And I proceeded to where things were chaotic.

And I saw there something horrible: I saw neither a heaven above nor a firmly founded earth, but a place chaotic and horrible.

And there I saw seven stars of the heaven bound together in it, like great mountains and burning with fire.

Then I said: "For what sin are they bound, and for what account have they been cast in hither?"

Then said Uriel, one of the holy angels, who was with me, and was chief over them, and said: "Enoch, why dost thou ask, and why art thou eager for the truth?

These are of the number of the stars of heaven which have transgressed the commandment of the Lord, and are bound here till ten thousand years, the time entailed by their sins, are consummated."

And from thence I went to another place, which was still more horrible than the former, and I saw a horrible thing: a great fire there which burned and blazed, and the place was cleft as far as the abyss, being full of great descending columns of fire: neither its extent or magnitude could I see, nor could I conjecture.

Then I said: "How fearful is the place and how terrible to look upon."

Then Uriel answered me: "Enoch, why hast thou such fear and affright?"

> And I answered: "Because of this fearful place, and because of the spectacle of the pain."
> And he said to me: "This place is the prison of the angels, and here they will be imprisoned forever."

The seven angels are described here as **'seven stars...like great mountains and burning with fire'**. We already saw that in Revelation 17, the Beast had seven heads and ten horns. We were told that the seven heads were seven mountains. They were also seven kings. So we see that these seven mountains are figures or metaphors for these seven stars or angels who transgressed the commandment of the Lord and are bound in this fearful place until they are released at the time of the Apocalypse.

It is important to reiterate that Jude, one of the sons of Mary and Joseph, quoted directly from this most ancient of books. For this gives the writings of Enoch gravitas and kudos and informs us that it is indeed an important book from which we can learn. To those who would say that if it is inspired, then it would already be included in the canon of scripture, I would reply that too often we are inclined to 'put God in a box'. Perhaps the Almighty did not want this book included at this time but rather kept it separate so that some new revelation could be gleaned from it in these, the Last Days. For I have found nothing in the Book of Enoch that contradicts anything in scripture. Rather, it complements the revealed Word of truth.

Regarding the fallen angels, the Book of Enoch, 6:1,2, has much to say:

> "And it came to pass when the children of men had multiplied that in those days were born unto them beautiful and comely daughters. And the angels, the children of heaven, saw and lusted after them, and said one to another: "Come, let us choose us wives from among the children of men and beget us children."

This concurs with the record in Genesis 6: 1,2 (KJV) which says:

> "And it came to pass, when men began to multiply on the face of the earth, and daughters were born unto them,
>
> That the sons of God saw the daughters of men that they were fair; and they took them wives of all that they chose."

Reverting back to Enoch we read:

> And Semjaza, who was their leader, said unto them: "I fear ye will not indeed agree to do this deed, and I alone shall have to pay the penalty of a great sin." And they all answered him and said: "Let us all swear an oath, and all bind ourselves by mutual imprecations not to abandon this plan but to do this thing."
>
> And they were in all 200 who descended in the days of Jared on the summit of Mount Hermon... And these are the names of their leaders: Semiazaz, Arakiba, Rameel, Kokabiel, Tamiel, Ramiel, Danel, Ezeqeel, Baraqiel, Asael, Armaros, Batarel, Ananel, Zaqiel, Samsapeel, Satarel, Turel, Jomjael, Sariel." These were their chiefs of tens." Book of Enoch 6: 1-6

It was during the lifetime of Jared that these Nephilim fell from heaven, fell from grace and fell to earth. Jared was born circa 3544BC. This was almost 1200 years before the Flood which occurred in 2348BC. Therefore these angels, the children of heaven, were on this earth for a thousand years or more which gave them ample time to corrupt and infect the DNA of the whole population of the earth to the point that:

> "The Lord saw how great man's wickedness on the earth had become, and that every inclination of the thoughts of his heart was only evil all the time."
> Gen 6:5 (KJV)

Enoch says that these angels, whom he later calls the Watchers, descended on Mount Hermon which is near the border of Palestine and Lebanon. Enoch goes on to fill in more blanks not provided in scripture.

> "And all the others together with them took unto themselves wives...and they began to go in unto them and to defile themselves with them...And they became pregnant and they bare great giants...who consumed all the acquisitions of men. And when men could no longer sustain them, the giants turned against them and devoured mankind...And to devour one another's flesh and to drink the blood." Book of Enoch 7:1-6

Enoch also informs us that these Watchers **'...taught them charms and enchantments and the cutting of roots and made them acquainted with plants'**. This is an obvious reference to black magic and the practices of the occult and now we know from whence it is derived. Is it not interesting that this same evil practice is present today and is the fastest growing religion and is gaining adherents all over the world? In many of the covens that indulge in such pursuits, the offering and drinking of blood is an important and necessary ingredient. Indeed there are many movies and TV programmes based on vampires and it would seem Hollywood is endeavouring to make this practice mainstream. Perhaps this ritual will become common again during the Apocalypse and this is why it is being promoted so widely now?

In addition to the 19 leaders referenced earlier, another, a 20th leader is mentioned: Azazel. Speaking of him some of the righteous angels say:

> "Thou seest what Azazel hath done, who hath taught all unrighteousness on earth and revealed the eternal

> secrets which were preserved in heaven. And they have gone to the daughters of men upon the earth and have slept with the women, and have defiled themselves and revealed to them all kinds of sin.
>
> And the women have borne giants, and the whole earth has thereby been filled with blood and unrighteousness." Book of Enoch 9:1-11

Once again we see that Enoch matches the record as given in Genesis and elsewhere which tells us that giants roamed the earth in those bygone days and these were the hybrid offspring of the fallen angels and human women.

> "And the Lord said: "Bind Azazel hand and foot and cast him into the darkness and make an opening in the desert, which is in Dudael, and cast him therein.
>
> And on the day of the great judgement he shall be cast into the fire.
>
> And the whole earth has been corrupted through the works that were taught by Azazel: to him ascribe all sin..."
>
> Destroy the children of fornication and the children of the Watchers...
>
> Go bind Semjaza and his associates who have united themselves with women so as to have defiled themselves with them in all their uncleanness...
>
> In those days shall they be led off to the Abyss of fire and to the torment and the prison in which they shall be confined forever." Book of Enoch 10:4,6,8,11,13

These passages from the Book of Enoch further show that the fallen angels of Genesis 6 are indeed locked up in an abyss to await a future judgment. It also tells us that these Watchers from heaven took human women to wife who in turn gave birth to giants. These evil spirit men taught humans the secrets of the occult and the casting of charms. They also introduced the sacrificing and drinking of human blood.

Many other passages in the Book of Enoch provide us with information that is merely alluded to in scripture. It introduces us to the leader of the Nephilim to which is ascribed all sin whose name is given as Azazel. This name crops up in the Bible in Leviticus 16:8,10 and 26 where it is translated, **'scapegoat'**. But Azazel is a proper name and should have been thus translated.

> "And Aaron shall cast lots upon the two goats; one lot for the Lord and the other for Azazel." Lev 16:8 (KJV)

Enoch refers to these fallen angels as **'stars', 'spiritual beings'** and **'Watchers'**. The term **'watcher'** appears in Daniel 4:13,17 and 23 in the KJV where it is referring to angels, messengers of God who came from heaven to earth.

> "I saw in the visions of my head upon my bed, and behold a watcher and a holy one came down from heaven." Dan 4:13 (KJV)

Here is yet another passage from Enoch 28:11ff which parallels truths we have already covered in scripture.

> "And I saw a deep abyss...I saw seven stars like great burning mountains and when I enquired regarding them the angel said: "This place is the end of heaven and earth: this has become a prison for the stars and the host of heaven...Here shall stand the angels that have connected themselves with women...And the women also of the angels who went astray shall become sirens.
>
> And I, Enoch, alone saw the vision, the ends of all things: and no man shall see as I have seen."

Once again we have a reference here to 'seven stars like burning mountains' which accords with Revelation 17 which speaks of seven mountains who are seven kings. There is also a verse in Revelation that speaks of, **'a great mountain burning with fire was cast into the sea, and the third part of the sea became blood'**. (Rev. 8:8 KJV) Most commentators think this is a reference to a volcano that is to erupt and fall into the sea during the Apocalypse. But this 'great mountain burning with fire' may be a metaphor referring to one of these fallen angels.

Also mentioned here are, **'the women of the angels who went astray'**, referring to them as sirens. In Greek mythology, sirens were women or winged creatures who lured unwary sailors onto the rocks and shipwreck. We already pointed out that female angels with wings like a stork are mentioned just once in scripture in Zechariah 5. So the Book of Enoch informs us and reaffirms that there are indeed female angels. When we read in Genesis 1, **'So God created man in His own image, in the image of God created He him, male and female created He them'**, it would appear that both men and women look like male and female angels. Except that the one place where female angels do appear in scripture, they are described as having wings. In many ancient relief's we see depictions of female angels having great wings.

Among the pantheon of Greek and Roman gods were goddesses namely, Hera, Demeter and Athena. One of the seven ancient wonders of the world was the Temple of Athena in Ephesus. It contained a huge 70 foot statue of the goddess made of pure gold. The Temple acted as a vault. Athena is shown having wings and bears a spear and a shield while a serpent glides in the background. There is a female entity mentioned in the Old Testament called the Queen of Heaven. There may be a connection to this female and the sirens that Enoch spoke of.

But for now we see that it is abundantly clear from the writings of Enoch that evil angels manifested themselves on the earth in those antediluvian days and married human women. Their interference with humankind in those days caused the whole world to become full of sin and violence and bloodshed which brought on the Flood of Noah. Because of their sin, the fallen angels or Nephilim, have been incarcerated in the Abyss or Tartarus to await a final day of judgment. But before that day, the pit of the Abyss must be opened and these spirits released into the earth once more to wreak havoc during the coming Apocalypse.

CHAPTER 14

# Azazel and the Post Flood Nephilim

MANY YEARS AGO, I remember reading what I thought was a very odd verse of scripture. It is in Ezekiel 23 and it is talking of two sisters who prostitute themselves. The two sisters are metaphors for Samaria and Jerusalem. As with many prophecies, these appear to have duel meanings and contain literal truths. Speaking of the promiscuity of one of the sisters it says:

> "There she lusted after her lovers, whose genitals were like those of donkeys and whose emissions was like that of horses." Ezekiel 23:20 (NIV)

I can remember reading this quite a few years ago and for some peculiar reason, the image stuck in my head (if you will excuse the pun). On reading the Book of Enoch several years later, that passage came to mind again. In it Enoch describes a vision he has of the fallen angels descending to earth and having marital relations with human women. This passage contains metaphors where bulls and cows (oxen) refer to men and women.

> "And again I saw with mine eyes as I slept, and I saw the heaven above, and behold a star fell from heaven, and it arose and ate and pastured among those oxen.
> And again I saw in the vision, and looked towards the heaven, and behold I saw many stars fall and cast themselves down from heaven to the first star, and they became bulls amongst those cattle and pastured with them.
> And I looked at them and saw, and behold they all let out their privy members, like horses, and began to cover the cows of the oxen, and they all became pregnant and bare elephants, camels and asses.
> And they began moreover to devour those oxen; and behold, all the children of the earth began to tremble and to quake before them and to flee from them."
> Book of Enoch 86:1,3,4,6

As with many places in scripture, the angels are called here 'stars'. The stars fall from heaven and cast themselves down to earth. This proves once more that what we are dealing with are fallen angels who come from this other parallel world called heaven. These are 'the fallen ones' and when they cover the females, they bare what Enoch calls elephants, camels and asses. In other words, they bare monsters who bore little resemblance to the humans.

These are the giants of the Old Testament and of the many myths and legends which speak of giants from every corner of the world. Even in my own country of Ireland, giants are mentioned several times in historical records. Balor was the famous one-eyed giant or Cyclops, who fought at the battle of Moytura. Close to my cottage on the side of a hill in the west of Ireland there is a mound made of stones which is referred to locally as, 'the grave of the giant'.

Sir William Wilde, father of the playwright Oscar Wilde, wrote two books on the history of Ireland. In one he speaks of five brothers who were the high kings of Ireland in an era perhaps 1700BC. One of these kings was named Genan. Wilde describes the most ancient of writing ever found in Ireland which was on a stone plaque placed in a wall in the County of Mayo. He has a sketch of this in his book with a footnote of the translation of the plaque which stated:

> "Here lies Genan, king of Ireland which was found in a tomb near the church of Breaffy, in the County of Mayo. And inside the tomb was a skeleton 12.5 feet in length."

There are other mentions of giants in many localities all over the island of Ireland, the Giants Causeway in County Antrim being the most famous. The most ancient history of Ireland is recorded in several books entitled, *The Annals of the Four Masters,* which also mentions giants in Ireland and says they made their livelihood by piracy and were very troublesome in the world in those days. It also names several giants which includes Genan and his brothers.

But I digress. The giants Enoch speaks of were the offspring of the Nephilim prior to the Flood of Noah. But there was a second irruption of fallen angels with women AFTER the Flood and the giant offspring of these are recalled several times in scripture. For instance, when Moses sent in 12 spies to reconnoitre the Promised Land, they returned and explained how that the whole area was filled with giants. Compared to these giants, they said, the Israelites looked like grasshoppers.

When Enoch says that the angels had privy members which were like those of horses, this ties in with the passage quoted from Ezekiel where the prophet describes the men of Egypt **'whose genitals were like that of donkeys and whose emissions were like that of horses'**. Surely both these prophets are speaking of the same men. Interestingly, there are many ancient friezes on the walls of various tombs and sarcophagi all over Egypt depicting men with privy members like those of horses.

I have some pictures of these in my book, *The Nephilim and the Pyramid of the Apocalypse* and also have several in a DVD I did entitled *The Return of the Nephilim.* One famous Egyptian picture shows a smiling man who is adorned in the dress of the gods. He has indeed a protruding privy member that is similar to that of a horse. The caption tells us that this is the god Min. I was tempted to add that if this was Min, one might only wonder what his brother, Max, looked like! But on a serious note, these pre-flood fallen angels had privy members like horses. So I presume that when they emerge again in the Apocalypse, they will be similarly endowed.

Speaking of a righteous angel who came to capture the fallen stars, Enoch continues:

> "And I saw one of those four (angels) who had come forth first, and he seized the first star that had fallen from the heavens, and bound it hand and foot and cast it into an abyss: now that abyss was narrow and deep, and horrible and dark.
>
> And as I was beholding in the vision, lo, one of the four who had come forth stoned them from heaven, and gathered and took all the great stars whose privy members were like those of horses, and bound them all hand and foot and cast them in an abyss of the earth." Book of Enoch 88:1,3

It should be blindingly obvious at this juncture to see that these fallen stars from heaven, who were captured and cast into the Abyss for the evil they perpetrated in those days, are the same spirits that Jesus visited in his risen spiritual body after his resurrection. So these angels got a surprise visitor some 2,380 years after being incarcerated about the time of the Flood which occurred circa 2,348BC.

Very little information is provided in scripture pertaining to the Nephilim or fallen ones of Genesis 6 and after. In this regard, Enoch fills in many of the gaps and provides lots of pieces of the jig-saw puzzle. It is only because the Book of Enoch is directly quoted in scripture that we relay it here. It proves much of what has been presented thus far and gives us the bigger picture as to the happenings of those bygone days of yore. Truly those were violent and evil times which spanned as much as a 1,000 years to the point that speaking of mankind it states:

> "And God saw the wickedness of man that it was great in the earth, and that every imagination of the thoughts of his heart was only evil continually. And it repented the Lord that he had made man on the earth and it grieved him in his heart. And the Lord said, " I will destroy man whom I have created from the face of the earth; both man and beast and the creeping thing and the fowls of the air; for it repenteth me that I have made them". Gen 6:5-7 (KJV)

It seems that demons are different to angels. Enoch says the demons that inhabit the world are those spirits that remained on earth after the giants, which are the hybrid products of spirits mating with humans, were drowned in the Flood. Thus these demons need a body to possess and they are responsible for much of the oppression and evil that exists in the world since the days of Noah.

One more point from the book of Enoch. In speaking of the Watchers or fallen angels, he says that they have the ability to change their forms. This may account for those weird looking beings we see in the reliefs in Egypt and elsewhere which show men with curious visages such as the god Horus. He has a man's body and the head of a falcon. Or the god Thoth which has the head of an ibis. These are birds and this may relate to those scriptures which refer to fallen angels as 'unclean and hateful birds' (Rev 18:2).

This reminds me of a story told to me a few years back by a man who works for the European office of this publishing house, Ambassador International, in Belfast, Ireland. This man is married to an Indonesian girl whose father has been a pastor in Jakarta for many years. There had been a lot of occultic activity going on in the islands where he worked. He was in his study late one night on his computer composing a letter encouraging his flock to pray and read their Bibles and be strong in the Lord. He remembered getting a strange odour. Then when he looked up, there was an attractive young man sitting in a chair across the room. He began to remonstrate with the aged minister telling him that these islands were under his control and to not be preaching the Word of God in this area. The pastor opened his Bible and began to read from one of the Gospels. At this, the young man got very annoyed and stood up shouting at the preacher. The pastor looked down and saw that the young man did not have feet but instead had talons like those of a bird of prey. Then there was a loud bang and the lights went out in the house and the man disappeared. But the old minister's computer remained on and he did not lose his letter.

CHAPTER 15

# War in Heaven: Earth Invaded

THE DAY OF WRATH is one of the main names given to the time of tribulation also called the Day of the Lord. To nail down this concept so as we are in no doubt as to what this term means, we use one of the main means of scripture interpretation; prior usage. That is, we examine where phrases or words are used before in order to establish what the exact meaning is.

In this regard, let us listen to what is said by the prophets of old concerning the Day of Wrath. Joel 2:30-31 (KJV) says:

> "And I shall show wonders in the heavens and in the earth, blood and fires and pillars of smoke. The sun shall be turned into darkness and the moon into blood, before the great and terrible Day of the Lord come."

Isaiah gives it thus:

> "Behold the Day of the Lord cometh cruel both with WRATH and fierce anger to lay the land desolate: and he shall destroy the sinners thereof out of it. For the stars of heaven and the constellations thereof shall not give their light: the sun shall be darkened in his

going forth, and the moon shall not cause their light to shine.

And I shall punish the world for their evil and the wicked for their iniquity and I will cause the arrogance of the wicked to cease and will lay low the haughtiness of the terrible.

Therefore I will shake the heavens and the earth shall remove out of her place in the WRATH of the Lord of hosts and in the day his fierce anger." Isaiah 13:9-13 (KJV)

In an earlier chapter we saw how that when the bottomless pit was opened, black smoke ushered forth from it and caused the light from the sun to become darkened. The Abyss now opened means that the fallen angels who were incarcerated there are to be released into the earth once again to wreak their havoc. Now consider how this ties in with a similar prophecy yet to come as recalled by the seer in Revelation 6:12-17 (KJV).

"And behold when he opened the sixth seal, and lo there was a great earthquake: and the sun became black as sackcloth of hair and the moon became as blood.

And the stars of heaven fell unto the earth, even as a fig tree casting her untimely figs when she is shaken of a mighty wind.

And the heavens departed as a scroll when it rolled together: and every mountain and island were moved out of their places.

And the kings of the earth, and the great men and the rich men, and the chief captains, and the mighty men and every bondman and every freeman hid themselves in the dens and in the rocks of the mountains.

> And said to the mountains and rocks, "Fall on us and hide us from the face of Him that sits on the throne and from the wrath of the Lamb.
>
> For the great Day of His Wrath is come and who shall be able to stand?"

We surmised earlier that the smoke from the pit of the Abyss is a literal smoke that may indeed blot out the sun and be the precursor for the emergence of the Antichrist from his hiatus in Tartarus. And in the opening of the sixth seal we are told that the sun will become black and the moon will turn blood red. It would appear that these verses concur with Joel and Isaiah who foretold of the coming of the Day of Wrath in a similar fashion.

A cataclysmic shaking of the earth will result in what sounds like a volcanic eruption, the smoke of which blots out the light of the sun and causes the moon to become red. Thus the angels who are locked up in the Abyss are released and these evil spirit men are free to begin their destruction. But wait. Could this same event herald another celestial incident resulting in the expulsion of the remainder of the rebel angels from the heavenly domain? For we note from this last passage in Revelation 6:13, that the stars fell from heaven unto the earth, even as:

> "... late figs drop from a fig-tree when shaken by a strong wind..." Rev 6:13 (NIV)

'Stars', as already noted, are a figure of speech meaning angels. Regular stars do not drop to earth. But these 'stars' fall from heaven to earth as figs drop from a fig tree, shaken by a mighty wind. It begs the question, what could cause these angels to fall to earth from heaven? We look to chapter 12:7-9 (NIV) for more evidence as to what may well be the case.

> "And there was war in heaven: Michael and his angels fought against the dragon; and the dragon and

> his angels fought back. But he (the dragon) was not strong enough, and they lost their place in heaven.
> The great dragon was hurled down-that ancient serpent called the Devil or Satan, who leads the whole world astray. He was hurled to the earth and his angels with him."

This is not a battle, but a war. And it is between two sets of warring spirit men who are here called angels. Michael is the archangel who is responsible for military action in the spiritual realm. He and his good angels war against the one third of the evil angels that rebelled with and are under the control of the ancient serpent, Satan.

We know the number of rebel angels is one third because verse 4 tells us; **'His tail swept a third of the stars (angels) out of the sky and flung them to the earth'**. These are the same stars that fall to the earth like figs dropping from a fig tree. What an image this evokes.

Most commentators teach that Satan and his band of evil spirits were expelled from heaven eons ago after his unsuccessful coup to usurp the Throne of God. Revelation 6 verse 10 (NIV) tells us:

> "For the accuser of our brothers, who accuses them before our God day and night, has been hurled down."

'Accuses' here is in the present tense. Apparently, Satan spends a lot of his time rehearsing the sins of Christians before the face of God 'day and night'.

In the City of God which is called Mount Zion lives the Most High God. On His right hand is His Son, the Lord Jesus Christ. They are surrounded by the 24 elders on their thrones. Then we have the myriads of good angels of whom Gabriel and Michael are the best known to us. This is the house Jesus spoke of when he told His disciples, **'In my Father's house are many mansions. I go to prepare a place for you'**.

At some remove from this hallowed city we have the Devil and his motley crew of evil spirit men. They live there and Satan, who is the accuser, spends a lot of his time accusing the brethren before God. Christians are 'the brethren'. Of course we also know that the Devil spends time going up and down earth like a lion, **'seeking whom he may devour'**. (1 Peter 5:8 KJV)

So what occurs in heaven that might cause a seismic shift in power and authority resulting in defeat in this future war, for the serpent and his hordes, occasioning them to fall to earth? Could it be what is called the Marriage Feast of the Lamb?

There is to be a future wedding to take place in heaven. The bride is the Church of God who are the born from above spirit filled believers who are members of the Body of Christ. The Messiah promised his disciples that one day he would return from heaven and take them to the place he was going to. Because the bridegroom is returning to receive his bride and take her to the marriage feast which is to take place in heaven, we have no need to fear the Day of Wrath or the coming Apocalypse.

At present, because we are human and frail, we sin. All men are liars and fall short of the glory of God. So the adversary has plenty of ammunition when it comes to accusing the believers before God day and night. But when the Messiah returns briefly to catch away His Church, then we become immortal and receive a new spiritual body like unto his immortal body. With the putting on of this new body, the old impurities of the flesh and blood sinner is no more. We become the pure and chaste bride of the Messiah and will be without sin.

As such, now Satan cannot accuse us anymore before God. And with the arrival of all the Christians who are the saved of God from Pentecost down through the ages to this time, space will become scarcer in heaven. God and His son will not put up with His bride being blasphemed in their presence anymore. So the Dragon and his entourage must go. War ensues and Satan and one third of the angels of heaven who sided with him, are ejected. They fall to earth like figs falling from a fig tree. The wrath of the Devil will be soon coming after his demise. Thus is fulfilled the prophetic utterance of Jesus in Luke 10:18 (KJV) when he said;

> "I beheld Satan as lightening falling to earth."

We are given a stark and dire warning from John the Revelator in this same chapter 12 and verse 12:

> "But woe to the earth and the sea, because the Devil has gone down to you. He is filled with fury, because he knows that his time is short." Rev 12:12 (NIV)

As we mentioned earlier, the city know as Mystery Babylon will become a haven and dwelling place for evil, vile spirits and demons, as will Jerusalem. This chapter 12 records the eviction of the Devil and his angels from the heavenly realm and their exile to an earth caught up in the emerging Apocalypse. This is why this world will become a literal, hell on earth. We do not know how many evil angels exactly will become manifest on the earth. But we are told that 'myriads' of good angels surround the Throne of God in heaven. One third of the angels made a determined and free will decision to side with Satan in order to defeat the Most High in the original rebellion. Therefore there will be a huge number of fallen angels arriving on planet earth after the departure of the Church. They will join with the 200 Nephilim who ascend from the Abyss under the leadership of the Beast.

When these evil fallen angels are cast out of heaven, which is a spiritual realm, they will, I believe, lose some of their inherent abilities and become manifest in this realm of the material. It is my feeling that they will be invisible no more and will be in plain sight for all to see.

As I touched on in a previous chapter, huge amounts of movies and books and TV shows concerning extraterrestrial activities are swamping the globe. It seems that every other TV programme or movie has a spiritual, magical, occult, mystical dimension, depicting beings coming from outer space to earth. UFO sightings and abductions are happening in their thousands every year. The human psyche is being bombarded with this information on a daily basis. The reason for this is simple to explain. For the Devil and his princes know they will shortly be cast down and consigned to earth to begin the last lap before their eternal damnation. So they must prepare the world and the natural man for their soon appearing so that it is not such a shock when it happens, as it might otherwise be. Unbeknown to themselves, those whose names are not written in the Lamb's Book of Life are being conditioned for the manifestation of these supernatural beings from above.

Many of the movies and TV programmes today are filled with gruesome and explicit and gratuitous violence and sex as well as filthy and repulsive language. Thus the human psyche becomes desensitised and inured to hard-core violence. This, I believe, is to prepare them for the bloodshed and inhumanity they will perpetrate during the Great Tribulation on their fellow human beings.

Besides these overt, in-your-face attempts at brainwashing via Hollywood etc., there are subtle and subliminal messages coming from the highest offices in the land. For instance, just recently, a telescope was launched into outer space from NASA to look for signs of life on other planets. This costing millions of dollars while thousands are dying daily for want of a little food and clean water. And for years we have been sending radio signals into space in the hope of receiving a response from intelligent alien life. This programme is called SETI- the search for extraterrestrial intelligence. Often scientists are heard on the air-waves saying that there has to be life on other planets given the size of the universe. Even the Roman Catholic Church have recently come out to state that there are alien beings in outer space but they are benign as they have been created by the same God that created humans. All these feed into the psyche of the human race and all are designed to prepare the world for the appearance of the gods who are to come.

It is imperative that we all play our part in warning others as to the calamity that awaits them if they refuse to accept salvation while there is still time. God would have all men saved and to come to a knowledge of the truth. Jesus Christ is their ticket out of here so that they are saved from the coming Wrath. Words could not describe, nor can we imagine, how bad the situation will be for those good people who will inevitably be trapped in this coming annihilation. But John provides a hint:

> "But woe unto the earth...because the Devil is gone down to you. He is filled with fury, because he knows his time is short." Rev 12:12 (NIV)

## Chapter 16
# Deceiving Spirits in the Church

I would like to take an in-depth look at the second chapter of the second epistle of Paul to the saints at Thessalonica. This is very important in assessing the timing of the emergence of the Beast from the Abyss into the world and when the gathering together of the Church will happen. I could spend a lot of time getting into definitions of Greek words and quoting from learned scholars who have done much research on this section. But too much technical information can overburden the reader. So I shall distil the research and provide enough evidence to prove our conclusions are accurate and true. I will dissect this chapter verse by verse and then tie it all together in a conclusion at the end, with the help of God. We begin at 2 Thessalonians, chapter 2, verse 1 (KJV):

> " Now we beseech you brethren, by the coming of our Lord Jesus Christ, and by our gathering together unto him."

Paul is addressing two issues here in this first sentence. First, **'the coming of our Lord'**, and secondly, **'our gathering**

**together unto Him'**. These are two separate events and must be distinguished as such. The coming of Jesus Christ back to earth to rule is going to occur at the end of the Apocalypse which culminates at Armageddon. After this, Jesus will establish His millennial Kingdom where He will rule this earth for one thousand years.

The gathering together, on the other hand, will occur before the events of the Great Tribulation begin and this will become clearer as we advance through this chapter.

Paul uses the word 'beseech' in his opening line. This is a very strong word in the Greek and means to 'earnestly beg' or 'to implore'. It is an extreme use of 'beg'. So what is Paul earnestly begging of the believers in Thessalonica?

> "That ye be not soon shaken in mind or be troubled, neither by spirit, nor by word, nor by letter, as from us, as that the day of Christ is at hand."

Here Paul explains what he is referring to. He is talking about 'the Day of Christ'. As was explained at the beginning of this opus, the 'Day of Christ' is another phrase meaning the 'Day of Wrath' or the 'Day of Judgement' or the 'Day of the Lord'. In other words, it is talking about the Great Tribulation and the incidents which are to occur during this awful time.

Paul says they are not to be shaken in mind or troubled. Again these are very extreme words which illustrate that the believers were terrified and their minds and hearts were under extreme pressure as a result of something they had heard. What it was that had them in this frightened state of mind which caused them undue pressure was that, **'the day of Christ is at hand'.** In the Greek, 'at hand' means, 'present'. That is, they were terrified because they thought the time of the Apocalypse was present or had begun, and they were to go through it.

Scholars agree that the NASB has the most accurate translation of this verse:

> "That you may not be quickly shaken from your composure or be disturbed either by a spirit or by a message or a letter as if from us, to the effect that the Day of the Lord has come."

Paul is earnestly beseeching them, begging them, not to be upset or worried that the Day of Wrath had begun. He said they were not to be troubled either by a spirit, nor by word, nor by letter from anyone, that this Day of Christ had begun. He continues:

> "Let no man deceive you by any means: for that day shall not come, except there come a falling away first, and that man of sin be revealed, the son of perdition."

It is interesting that Paul tells them, **'let no man deceive you...'** for there is so much deception going on in evangelical circles today regarding this topic. But here we will ignore what man says and adhere only to the Word of truth and allow it speak on its own behalf as we have from page one of this book. For if we stay on the narrow path of the Word, then our passage will be sure and true.

We are not to allow ourselves be deceived by any man or by a spirit (an evil spirit of deception), working through man; **'for that day shall not come, except there come a falling away first'**. 'That day' is again referring to the Day of Wrath or the Great Tribulation. And that day cannot begin 'except there come a falling away first'. So after this falling away, then the Day of Wrath can commence and when it does, then shall **'that man of sin be revealed, the son of perdition'**.

Paul is telling us not to allow ourselves to be tricked by any man into believing that the Day of Wrath has begun, for it cannot start until after a 'falling away'. Then when it does start, the man of sin, the son of perdition or Antichrist, will be revealed. But not until AFTER the 'falling away'. So what is this 'falling away'? For this is the key phrase which points to the commencement of the Apocalypse and the revealing of the Beast from the Abyss.

The Greek for 'falling away' is *apostasia.* This word has been transliterated into the English as 'apostasy' which means an abandonment of one's religious faith. Thus the vast majority of Biblical teachers and students believe that in these Last Days, Christians and believers of all hues will turn away from God and from the truths of the Bible and fall by the wayside. Almost every evangelical teacher believes there will be a 'falling away' from God in the End Times, and you can read this in books and periodicals and on websites everywhere. They point to the hedonistic ways of the world and to the downward spiral of depravity into which the secular world is going. And they use this to prove that the apostasy is occurring. But this is not the original meaning of the word *apostasia* in early Greek literature.

Firstly, in the text it reads 'THE' falling away and not, 'a' falling away as it reads in the King James Version. This is a crucial difference. This marks out 'the falling away' as a specific event.

*Apostasia* is made up of two words, *apo* and *stasia.* In appendix 104 of *The Companion Bible*, EW Bullinger defines the various Greek prepositions and what they mean. Greek is a mathematical language and is very precise. He defines *apo* thus:

" *Apo* governs only one case, the genitive, and denotes motion from the surface of an object, as a line drawn from the circumference of an object...Hence it is used of *motion away* from a place. *Apo* may consequently be used of *deliverance* or *passing away from* a state or condition."

In Greek, *apo* can be represented as a line drawn starting from the circumference of a circle and going away in an outward direction. *Stasia* literally means a 'standing' or 'to draw out', or 'to separate'.

So the whole word means, 'a standing away from', or 'a drawing out from', or 'a separation away from', or 'a going out from among'. The original meaning of this word, which is agreed by many Greek scholars familiar with the ancient texts is, 'the departure'. This agrees with the definition of '*apo*' in Greek which suggests 'a motion from the surface' or 'a motion away from a place as a line drawn from the circumference of an object'.

The Geneva Bible, the Cranmer Bible, first published in 1537, the Tyndale Bible published in 1539, preceding the King James Version, all translate this verse, **'before the Day of the Lord comes, there must come a departure first'**. That is, before the Day of the Lord begins, there must first be a departure of the born-again believers from this world to be with Christ.

Paul Tan, a scholar, did an extensive study on the phrase, 'falling away', and had this to say:

> "What precisely does Paul mean when he says that the falling away must happen before the Tribulation? The definite article 'the' denotes that this is a definite event, an event distinct from the appearance of the man of sin. The Greek word for 'the falling away' taken by itself does not mean apostasy or defection. Neither does it mean 'to fall' as the Greeks have another word for that (*pipto*: I fall). The best translation of the word is, 'to depart'. The apostle Paul here refers to a definite event which he calls, 'the departure' which will occur just before the start of the Tribulation. This departure is the gathering together of the Church otherwise called by some, the Rapture of the Church."

Remember the context of this whole chapter:

1. The coming of the Lord Jesus.
2. Our gathering together unto Him.

So 'the departure' is referring to the gathering together of the Church of God. Paul had elaborated on this in length in his first epistle to the Thessalonians when he described how Jesus would come briefly and all Christian believers would be caught up or gathered to meet Him in the air. So what Paul is doing here is allaying their worst fears. For some people were teaching that the Day of the Lord, or Tribulation, had already begun and that they were to suffer through it. This is why their minds were shaken and they were greatly troubled and terrified. But Paul reiterates and reminds them that this time of Wrath *cannot* begin until first there is '*the* departure'. And only after that will the man of sin, the Antichrist, be revealed. This is why Paul says in verse 5:

> "Remember ye not that, when I was yet with you, I told you these things?"

He is reminding them that he already spelled out in great detail in his first letter that the Lord would return briefly to gather them together and he finished his passage in 1 Thessalonians 4:18 regarding the Rapture with the phrase:

> "Wherefore comfort one another with these words."

For there is no comfort in telling Christians that they are to suffer the horrible torture and persecution and death at the hands of the Devil's angels in the Great Tribulation. Jesus also stated this truth in John 14:1-4 (KJV) when He promised His disciples that He was going to His Father's house but would return for them:

> "Let not your heart be troubled; ye believe in God, believe also in me.
>
> In my Father's house are many mansions. If it were not so, I would have told you. I go to prepare a place for you.
>
> And if I go to prepare a place for you, I will come again and receive you unto myself, that where I am, there ye may be also."

Can anything be more plain? These are the words of Jesus Himself. He clearly states that He is going to prepare a place for us. He says this twice lest we are in any doubt. For why would He be preparing a place for us if we are to remain here on earth? By Jesus telling us that he is preparing a place for us in heaven, the inference is we are going to be spending some time there. When the time is right, he will return and take us to this house of many rooms. But listen to how the Lord begins this passage:

**'Let not your heart be troubled.'** This ties in with Paul's statements in both 1 Thess 4 and in 2 Thess 2 where he says, when speaking about the gathering together, **'Wherefore, comfort one another with these words'**, and also when he earnestly begged them, **'That ye be not soon shaken in mind or be troubled'**. Paul exhorted the Christians in his day not to be deceived by any man or by any spirit that may be operating through man. Or by letters or fine words from sincere people, even if they are Bible believing Christians. We are not going through the day of Wrath because the departure of the Christians MUST happen first, then and only then will the Tribulation begin and the man of sin, the Beast from the Abyss will be manifested.

> "Who opposes and exalts himself above all that is called God, or that is worshipped; so that he as God, sits in the Temple of God, showing himself that he is God." 2 Thess 2:4 (KJV)

This is what the Beast will do in the latter part of the Apocalypse. Commentators take from this that a new Temple will be built in Jerusalem and at some time near the end of the Tribulation, the Antichrist will go into the Temple and proclaim that he indeed is the one and only true God. The epistle continues:

> "And now ye know what witholdeth that he might be revealed in his time. For the mystery of iniquity doth already work: only he who now letteth will let,

> until he be taken out of the way. And then shall that wicked be revealed..." 2 Thess 2:6,7,8 (KJV)

'Witholdeth' and 'letteth' are both the same word in Greek, *katecho,* which means 'hold fast; hold back; to restrain from going; keep secure; keep firm; that which hinders.' This is speaking of the Antichrist. And Paul is literally saying, 'now you know what is holding him fast', or, 'there is one who is holding him fast', or 'he who now restrains'. This agrees with our study so far which has taught us that the Antichrist is in prison, or is being held fast, in an underground jail. And he will be held secure in this prison, **'until he be taken out of the way'**. What must be taken out of the way before the man of sin can be revealed? According to this chapter so far, there can be only one answer; The Church of God or Body of Christ must depart or be taken out of the way first, before the Antichrist can be released from the place where he is presently being 'held fast'.

The New International Version translates verse 6 so:

> "And now you know what is holding him (Antichrist) back, so that he may be revealed at the proper time."

It is not an apostasy that is holding the Antichrist back. If anything, an apostasy should hasten his arrival. It is the presence of the Holy Spirit indwelling the Church of God on this earth which is preventing the Beast from ascending out of the Abyss at this present time. But when the Church departs, then the man of sin will no longer be held back and will be revealed.

Imagine you are in the departure lounge of an airport. Then you get into the plane and it takes off. The plane goes in a motion away from the circumference of the earth as it ascends up into the air. This is 'the departure'. This is the meaning of *apostasia.* It has nothing to do with people turning away from God. For God promised that in the Last Days, He would pour out His spirit on His people.

> "And it shall come to pass in the last days, saith God, I will pour out in those days of my Spirit on all flesh: and your sons and your daughters shall prophesy, and your young men shall see visions, and your old men shall dream dreams: And on my servants and on my handmaidens I will pour out in those days of my Spirit; and they shall prophesy." Acts 2:17,18 (KJV)

This is evidenced by the fact that thousands are coming to Christ daily around the world and the Word is spreading rapidly, mostly in poorer countries such as Africa, South America and China as well as India.

Paul never mentions a rebellion or a falling away in Thessalonians. The whole context of the epistle is the gathering together, the Day of the Lord and the second coming. So there is no need to worry. Comfort your family and friends with these words. Jesus has promised us that He will return to take us to the place He has been preparing for us for the past 2,000 years. We have little to be fearful of or troubled about for He has spoken; '**Let not your hearts be troubled**'. Romans 5:9 (KJV) agrees with the thesis that the Church of God is not involved in the Tribulation:

> "Since we have now been justified by His blood, how much more shall we be saved from God's wrath through Him."

This truth is reiterated in 1 Thess 1:10 (NIV):

> "And to wait for His Son from heaven, whom He raised from the dead-Jesus, who rescues us from the coming wrath."

And again in 1 Thess 5:9 (NIV):

> "For God did not appoint us to suffer wrath, but to receive salvation through our Lord Jesus Christ."

How many times must we be told such comforting truths yet still so many refuse to accept and believe. The evil spirits that were operating to terrify Christians in Thessalonica are working hard in the Church today. You can believe these spirits if you so choose. But I believe the words of Jesus and of Paul.

CHAPTER 17

# 50 Prophecies of the Antichrist

PAUL ASSURES THE BELIEVERS in his letter to the Thessalonians that the Holy Spirit is 'holding fast' the Antichrist and that he will not be released until after the departure or gathering together of the saints. Verse 7:

> "For the secret power of lawlessness is already at work; but the one who now holds it back will continue to do so till he is taken out of the way.
>
> And then the lawless one will be revealed, whom the Lord Jesus will overthrow with the breath of His mouth, and will destroy by the splendour of His coming." 2 Thess 2:7,8 (NIV)

The secret power of lawlessness is the work of Satan and his princes who are not locked up as Apollyon is. They are orchestrating operations here on earth in preparation for the release of their friends from their gloomy dungeons. But God or the Holy Spirit are holding him in his present incarceration until 'he is taken out of the way'. That is, until the Body of Christ is gathered together and evacuated off this earth.

(This latter expression, 'taken out of the way', is used in Acts 17:33, 23:10, 1 Cor 5:2, 2 Cor 6:17, Col 2:12).

After the Rapture, the Antichrist will be released and at the end game of the Apocalypse, the Lord Jesus will return and destroy the Beast with the breath of His mouth and the splendour of His appearance. Then we are provided with a couple of more hints regarding the *modus operandi* of the Beast from the Abyss.

> "The coming of the lawless one will be in accordance with the work of Satan displayed in all kinds of counterfeit miracles, signs and wonders, and in every sort of evil that deceives those that are perishing. They perish because they refused to love the truth and so be saved." 2 Thess 2:9,10 (NIV)

As was pointed out previously, the Beast, when he arrives on the world stage, will perform signs, miracles and wonders and indulge in every evil imaginable. Many of the population of the world will be deceived by his sleight-of-hand because they want to indulge in sinful evil practices. As a result, they will perish because they refuse to love Jesus Christ and get saved in doing so. 2 Thess 2:11,12 (NIV):

> "For this reason God will send them a powerful delusion so that they will believe the lie and so that all will be condemned who have not believed the truth but have delighted in wickedness."

What is the lie they will be deluded into believing? Many evangelical Christians say that the doctrine of the Rapture is the lie that is being perpetrated today and is a delusion, for, they say, we must suffer the trials by enduring the Tribulation.

Firstly, this lie and delusion is only going to happen when the Antichrist is at large and working his lying signs, miracles and wonders. It is evidently clear that this is still in the future. Secondly, those who believe the lie are non Christians for they refuse to believe the truth but rather delight in their evil wickedness. This is hardly a description of Christians. So those who peddle this untruth are themselves deluded, methinks.

The lie that will be believed, I surmise, is that this man will put himself forward as the true Messiah, and the people of the world will accept him as the true Christ. This is why Jesus said in John 5:43 (KJV):

> "I am come in my Father's name, and ye receive me not: if another come in his own name, him ye will receive."

This is an obvious reference to the Antichrist who is to come. Jesus was rejected by the world and suffered and was crucified and died. Contrast this with the false Messiah who is to come and who will be accepted with open arms by most of the world who will pledge allegiance to him and accept his mark. This is why I think the great delusion is that the world will believe that this Antichrist is indeed, in the stead of the true Christ, and as such will embrace him as their saviour.

We have examined many aspects of the coming Beast from the bottomless pit, which will allow future readers of this work, who may find themselves caught in the Apocalypse, to identify the Beast. I will now provide 50 brief prophecies regarding the Antichrist, and where they appear in Scripture. The following was sent to me a few years ago and I am grateful to the anonymous author who compiled the list. Although I may not totally agree with every one of these, nevertheless the list is useful in that it gives a glossary of the prophecies concerning the Antichrist which can be surveyed at a glance. The original quotes are from the King James Version whereas my comments will appear in brackets.

## 50 PROPHECIES OF THE ANTICHRIST

1. The Antichrist is a man—Daniel 7:24,25

(Indeed the Antichrist is a man. However, he is not a human, flesh and blood man. Rather he is a spirit man as all angels who appear in Scripture are so described. Thus he can perform supernatural signs and wonders).

2. He will confirm a covenant for seven years—Daniel 9:27

(The Antichrist will broker a peace deal between the Jews and their Arab neighbours which, scholars say, will last seven years. Thus he is the rider on the white horse having a bow but no arrow).

3. He will arise among ten kings—Daniel 7:8

(That is, when the Beast ascends out of the Abyss, he will be accompanied be ten other kings and he will be their ruler. Seven other heads, who are also kings or rulers, will arise with these from the pit. These are all fallen angels as is the Antichrist).

4. This ten nation union will be a revived Roman Empire —Daniel 2:44

(This arises from the dream Nebuchadnezzar had which was interpreted by Daniel. The ten toes of iron are associated with the legs of iron which was the old Roman Empire. However, I believe the combined forces of the West, who are by and large, descendents of the Roman Empire, or Europe, will be the driving force behind the ten supranational government regions which will be a world-wide phenomenon).

5. He will uproot three kings—Daniel 7:8

(These three kings or rulers are the beast with two horns who is the False Prophet and two other fallen spirit men. We suggested this may be the prophesied and expected Imam al-Mahdi or 12th Imam on which the Muslim world awaits. The Antichrist may have to subdue or defeat the False Prophet and his two accomplices in order to get them 'on side'. Nevertheless these are three other fallen angels who are to arise from captivity out of the earth).

6. His ten nation union will merge into a world government which he will dominate—Revelation 13:1,2

(There is no doubt that this government is world-wide and is not confined to Europe alone which is a ridiculous idea propagated by many).

7. He will ascend to power on a platform of world peace and will by peace destroy many—Daniel 8:25

(This is represented by the rider on the white horse who has a bow but no arrow. He shall preach peace but wage war).

8. He will be promoted by a miracle working religious partner —Revelation 13:11,12

(This is the False Prophet or lamb with two horns (rulers), who is the beast who ascends out of the earth).

9. The beast was, and is not, and shall ascend out of the bottomless pit and go into perdition (destruction)—Revelation 17:8

(The Beast 'was', in the days of yore when he reigned along with the other fallen angels who were the gods of those days; 'and is not', because he is locked up in Tartarus with the rest of the evil spirits who fell to earth with him in those days; 'and shall ascend out of the bottomless pit and go into perdition'. Apollyon shall ascend out of his prison and begin his work which will end in mass destruction).

10. The world government over which the Antichrist rules will be a socialist government—Revelation 17:3

(The policies which are being implemented as we speak are of a global nature and make the ruling governments supreme and responsible for the welfare of the citizens from womb to tomb. The power is from the top down and not by the people, for the people and of the people. Therefore it is a socialist one-world agenda which is being instigated).

11. The Antichrist will be preceded by seven kings. He will be the eighth, and will be 'of' the seven—Revelation 17:11

(The Antichrist will not be preceded by seven kings, because we are told that when the Beast ascends, he will have 'seven heads and ten horns.' Therefore these seventeen kings or rulers will appear at the same time).

12. He will have a mouth speaking great things—Daniel 7:8

(This accords with 2 Thessalonians which says he will exalt himself above God. We may assume that the Antichrist will be an eloquent speechmaker who will be able to convince people by way of his great oratorical skills).

13. His look will be more stout than his fellows—Daniel 7:20

(The NIV says; 'The horn that looked more imposing than the others and that had eyes and a mouth that spoke boastfully'. So this is obviously going to be a striking individual who is extremely arrogant).

14. He will be of fierce countenance—Daniel 8:23

(The NIV says, 'a stern faced king', while the margin note in *The Companion Bible* gives; 'a king of mighty presence').

15. He will understand dark sentences—Daniel 8:23

(NIV; 'A master of intrigue,' while *The Companion Bible* notes; 'skilled in dissimulation'. Dissimulation means to hide something by pretence).

16. He will cause craft to prosper—Daniel 8:25

(Craft is deceit. So he will cause deceit to prosper which agrees with 2 Thessalonians and other places which tell us he will delude almost the whole world with his lying signs and wonders).

17. He apparently assumes world dominating power three and a half years after he confirms the covenant. He then will continue his reign 42 months—Revelation 13:5

(Many times we are told of a 42 month period being associated with the Antichrist and others in Revelation. Some argue that the whole Apocalypse is seven years long. Others say three and a half years and use verses like this to bolster their case).

18. The Abomination of Desolation is the event that signals the beginning of his final 42 months—Daniel 9:27

(The Antichrist will enter the rebuilt Temple and proclaim that he is God. This is the Abomination of Desolation. Whether there is 42 months left to go until Armageddon or not is moot).

19. He opposes God—2 Thessalonians 2:4

(He is literally God's adversary and is named as such in other places in Scripture).

20. He shall speak marvellous things against the God of gods—Daniel 11:36

(The NIV says; 'He will say unheard-of things against the God of gods').

21. He exalts himself above all that is called God—2 Thessalonians 2:4

(This is the New Testament according with the Old Testament).

22. He will sit in the Temple of God—2 Thessalonians 2:4

(Many believe that as a result of any peace deal between the Jewish nation and the Arabs, the Jews will be allowed rebuild the Temple in Jerusalem).

23. He claims to be God—2 Thessalonians 2:4

(Satan tried to usurp the Throne of God in ancient times and failed. This is his last attempt to proclaim that he is higher than the Most High God).

24. He will take away the daily sacrifice at the time of the Abomination of Desolation—Daniel 11:31

(The Antichrist will put a stop to the Jewish daily sacrifices and replace it with an abomination which will cause the desolation).

25. He shall plant the tabernacles of his palace between the seas in the glorious holy mountain—Daniel 11:45

(The NIV: 'He will pitch his royal tents between the seas at the beautiful holy mountain. Yet he will come to an end, and no-one will help him.' This is where the Antichrist meets his doom for Jesus will defeat him and he will be cast into the Lake of Fire).

26. It was given him to make war with the saints, and to overcome them—Revelation 13:7

(We have discussed this in some detail. He will hunt down and torture and kill the Christians who have turned to God in the time of the Tribulation).

27. He will make war with the saints three and a half years—Daniel 7:21,25

(Here is another reference to three and a half years. This tells those Christians how long they must endure before Jesus returns at the Battle of Armageddon).

28. The time of the Great Tribulation launched by the Antichrist begins at the Abomination of Desolation—Matthew 24:15,21

(Again this is in debate. For the Tribulation may be already on-going at this point).

29. During this time he will scatter the power of the holy people—Daniel 12:7

(Satan will go after the Jews when he is cast from heaven to earth. This is recorded in Revelation 12).

30. He will rule a terrible and strong kingdom—Daniel 7:7

(The Antichrist will rule the strongest and deadliest army the world has ever witnessed).

31. Power was given him over every tribe and people and tongues and nations—Revelation 13:7

(The Beast from the Abyss will reign over the kings of the earth and all nations and tribes and tongues will worship him).

32. His kingdom will devour the whole earth —Daniel 7:23

(Meaning his ten region geo-political union will encompass all the world and not just the European Union as some teach).

33. Arms shall stand on his part - Daniel 11:31

(This is reiterating that he will have a massive military power at his disposal).

34. He shall attack the mighty fortresses with the help of a foreign god—Daniel 11:39

('Foreign god' in Hebrew is *eloha-necher* which means 'alien god'. Thus, he will act against the strongest fortresses (world powers) with the help of an alien god which he shall acknowledge and advance its glory (in the eyes of the world), and he shall cause them (the alien gods), to rule over many, (the inhabitants of the world), and divide the land for gain (split it up into ten geo-political regions).

35. He will think to change times and laws: and they will be given into his hands for three and a half years—Daniel 7:25

(We can observe subtle changes already taking place in our world today. Christmas is being replaced with the 'Holiday Season' and in some cases the use of the word 'Christmas' is banned).

36. He shall prosper—Daniel 8:24

(Everything he does will appear to yield good results for the beginning of his reign. But the latter end will result in destruction world-wide).

37. He shall not regard the god of his fathers—Daniel 11:37

(He exalts himself above all other gods and above the Most High God).

38. He will not regard the desire of women—Daniel 11:37

(This is a most interesting phrase and seems to suggest that the Antichrist will be gay. For if he does 'not regard the desire of women', is it inferring that he does regard the desire of men? Of course in the secular world we live in, this would be applauded by the media and most people).

39. The mark of the beast will be the mark of his name—Revelation 14:11

(It would seem that the Mark of the Beast and the number of his name is a micro-chip placed under the skin of the right hand or on the forehead).

40. The number of the beast is 666—Revelation 13:18

(There are experiments already being carried out on families in the USA who have received chips under their skin. The EU is presently spending millions of Euro implementing a policy where all the information of its citizens is being computerised and the citizens will have a universal plastic card common to everyone in the European Union. It is but a small step from this to planting a chip under the skin).

41. 666 will be the number of his name—Revelation 15:2

(Of course to the natural man, it would seem a positive action if everybody would receive a chip on their person. For this would eliminate the need for cash which would in turn cut out illegal activities such as drug-dealing and bank robberies. It would also be acceptable to the governments as an excuse to combat terrorist activity).

42. All that dwell upon the earth shall worship him, except those whose names are written in the lamb's Book of Life—Revelation 13:8

(Those who turn to Jesus and God during the Tribulation will endure horrific hardship and death. But their names are written in the Lamb's Book of Life. These are the unwise virgins Jesus spoke about. But the majority of the peoples of the world will gladly worship the Beast and his promise to save the world, for people love darkness more than light).

43. The Antichrist will have an image—Revelation 15:2

(The False Prophet will erect an image of the Antichrist and will amaze the world by bringing this image to life. This is part of the lying signs and wonders which the Beast and the False Prophet will do in order to deceive the world into accepting them as their saviours).

44. His coming is after the coming of Satan—2 Thessalonians 2:9

(This leaves us in no doubt as to who the real power is behind the Beast. He receives his authority and power from Satan. The Antichrist and the False Prophet and Satan make up an infernal Trinity).

45. He will fight against Jesus Christ at Armageddon—Revelation 17:14

(He will gather together the kings of the earth to fight against the Lord Jesus who will appear with His chosen and called and faithful. This battle will begin at the Valley of Megiddo in Northern Israel and will be a world-wide conflagration).

46. He will stand against the Prince of princes—Daniel 8:25

(But he will lose and his future is in the Lake of Fire along with the False Prophet and the Devil).

47. The Lord will destroy him with the spirit of His mouth—2 Thessalonians 2:8

('Out of His mouth comes a two-edged sword', which is the Word of God).

48. The Lord will consume him with the splendour of His coming—2 Thessalonians 2:8

(When Jesus returns, He will be mounted on a white horse and His servants will accompany Him dressed in white linen and also riding horses. Oh, what a spectacle that will be and I hope I am among those riding behind my Lord and Saviour who is King of kings and Lord of lords).

49. The Beast is cast alive into the Lake of Fire—Revelation 19:20

(One thousand years after the Beast and the False Prophet are cast alive into the Lake of Fire, the Devil joins them there. This proves that both the Beast and the false Prophet are indeed spirit men or fallen angels. For Jesus told us the Lake of Fire was reserved for the Devil and his angels).

50. He will be tormented day and night for ever and ever—Revelation 20:10

(The Devil and his angels know the Bible better than you or I. They will do everything in their power to break the Word of prophecy and prevent its fulfilment. But the Most High God and His Son have the victory. It is but a matter of time before the great gathering together of the Church shall occur and then we are into the doomsday scenario of the start of the Apocalypse and the revealing of the Beast who will ascend out of the bottomless pit).

CHAPTER 18

# The Mystery and the Princes of Darkness

WHEN THE APOCALYPSE BEGINS, it will be the start of the most horrendous period in world history. It will make World War 1, World War 2, Hitler, Stalin, Pol Pot, Rwanda and all the other wars since the dawn of time, look like an afternoon tea-party. Famines and disease will be multiplied a thousand fold. Literally, the spawn of Satan will break loose to terrorise humankind.

So who will go through this tribulation? Are we all to suffer its effects? Or, as some teach, is there to be a group of favoured people who will avoid the coming cataclysm? To answer this vexed question, we begin with a statement by the Apostle Paul in 1 Corinthians 2:7,8 (KJV):

> "But we speak the wisdom of God in a MYSTERY, even the hidden wisdom which God ordained before the world unto our glory.
>
> Which none of the princes of this world knew: for had they known it, they would not have crucified the Lord of glory."

Paul here speaks of a mystery that had been hidden since before the beginning of the creation of the world. This mystery is of such import and magnitude, that had the **'princes of this world'** known about it, they would not have crucified Jesus Christ. So who are the 'princes of this world'? Well the chief prince is a person we have been discussing all through these writings. Jesus mentions him several times:

> "Now is the judgement of this world: now shall the prince of this world be cast out."
> John 12:31 (KJV)
> "Henceforth I will not talk much with you, for the prince of this world cometh, and hath nothing in me."
> John 14:30 (KJV)

Satan is referred to several times as the 'prince' of this world and the prince of devils. So the prices of this world are Satan and his fellow evil fallen angels.

So what is this mystery that it is so important? First mention of this great secret is given in the last chapter of the Epistle of Paul to Christian believers who lived in Rome.

> "Now to Him that is of power to establish you according to my gospel, and the preaching of Jesus Christ, according to the revelation of THE MYSTERY, which was kept secret since the world began, but now is made manifest, and by the scriptures of the prophets, according to the commandment of the everlasting God, made known to all nations for the obedience of faith." Romans 16:25,26 (KJV)

The word 'mystery' in the Greek literally means 'sacred secret'. According to Paul, this mystery had been kept secret since the world began, but was only now being revealed to all the nations via his writings. Paul further goes on to reveal what this sacred secret is in the epistle to the Ephesians chapter 3:3-6,8,9. (KJV).

> "How that by revelation He made known unto me the mystery...Which in other ages was not made known unto the sons of men and is now revealed unto His holy apostles and prophets by the Spirit;
>
> That the Gentiles should be fellow heirs and of the same body, and partakers of His promise in Christ by the gospel:
>
> Unto me... is this grace given, that I should preach among the Gentiles the unsearchable riches of Christ; And to make all men see what is the fellowship of the mystery, which from the beginning of the world hath been hid in God, who created all things."

Three times between Romans and Ephesians we are told that this sacred secret had been hidden in God since before the world was created. That is how important this mystery is. This mystery is in two parts. This first part reveals that the Gentiles were to be fellow heirs and of the same body, together with Israel, and partakers of the promises of Christ. That is, the Gentiles were now to share fully in the promises of God as provided for, by, and in Christ Jesus.

So what is the big deal with this, you might ask? Well for centuries before, from the time of Moses, the nation of Israel were the chosen people. Unto them was committed the Laws of God and the promises of God. As far as the Jews were concerned, the Gentiles, which meant everyone else, were mere dogs. They and only they, were the chosen ones. But now, as revealed by Paul, all this has changed. Now the Gentiles can receive the gift of Holy Spirit and as such, become co-equal with the Jews in all the promises of God.

But the second part of the great mystery is even more major than the first part. This is reiterated by Paul in Colossians 1:26-27 (KJV).

> "Even the mystery which had been hid for ages and from generations, but now is made manifest to His saints;

> To whom God would make known what is the riches of the glory of this mystery among the Gentiles, which is Christ in you, the hope of glory."

Prior to the giving of the Holy Spirit on the Day of Pentecost, the Gentiles were without hope and without God in this world. But now, because of His sacrifice and the shedding of the blood of Christ, all that is changed and changed utterly. This secret which no man knew of, for it was hidden by God since before the world began, is now revealed to Paul and made know to the nations. Not just that the Gentiles are now included in the family of God, but that everyone who believes gets eternal life and that life is, '**Christ in you, the hope of glory**'.

This is an incredible gift and an astounding revelation. So tremendous a revelation of this sacred secret is this; that if the princes of this world had known it, **'they would not have crucified the Lord of glory'**.

Just think about that for a moment. So stupendous and monumental and momentous is this revelation that, had Satan and the rest of the fallen angels known about it, they would not have murdered Jesus Christ on the cross. They would have preferred to have him still walking about the earth today than allow this miracle to happen. For when Jesus walked, He had the power of God's Holy Spirit in Him and He did mighty works. But he was one man working alone. But because of His crucifixion and subsequent resurrection, now that same Spirit has been made available to all who accept Jesus as their personal saviour and believe that God raised Him from the dead.

When you receive the Spirit of God in you, this is His seed and it is eternal life. Now you are going to heaven and all hell cannot stop you. When Jesus was on this earth, it was one man with the spirit and power of God in him. But about 3,000 more souls were added on the day of Pentecost. Then thousands more in the days and months that followed. Jesus said he was the 'light of the world'. Wherever the light goes, darkness has to flee. So every time another soul receives the gift of Holy Spirit, another light is lit in this perverted world and the darkness is banished. If you switch a light on in a room, darkness must vanish. Now there are millions of lights being turned on in countries all over the world.

The Jews were the servants of God and a few chosen ones used to receive the Spirit 'upon' them in Old Testament times. But this is no more. Now it is the eternal seed of God in you which makes you a son of God by birth, and you cannot lose that seed. And the great mystery, the sacred secret that was hidden in God from before the creation of the world, is that it is Christ in you, the hope of glory...Christ in you...What an amazing, literal truth. You have the spirit of Christ in you. That's the same Spirit that Christ received when John baptised him and the Spirit descended on him like a dove. And now it is inside you.

You can accomplish the same works as Jesus. As a son, you have direct access to the Throne of God in heaven. You can pray and preach and teach and cast out demons just as Jesus did, and the Devil does not like this one bit. And had he known this was going to happen, he and his princes would not have crucified Jesus. For now you have the same power of God residing in you and at your disposal. All you have to do is begin to act on what you have been given.

Because of this great mystery, Satan has worked over the centuries to diminish the teaching of this secret. Many Christian folks have no idea of its implications. It has been glossed over and ignored. But those of us who are born from above and have received the gift of God, are saved. We are now the Church, the *ekklesia* or called out of God and members of the Body of Christ. We are the saints which means we are sanctified or set apart. This is why the epistles are addressed to 'the saints at Rome', or 'the saints at Corinth', or 'the saints at Ephesus' etc. We are a special and unique group of people which God hid in His own heart since before the foundation of the world. No one knew about us but Him.

> "Praise be to God and the Father of our Lord Jesus Christ, who has blessed us in the heavenly realms with every spiritual blessing in Christ.
>
> For He chose us in him before the creation of the world to be holy and blameless in His sight."
>
> Eph 1:3,4 (NIV)

We are not servants but sons of God by birth and citizens of Heaven. This makes us different from the children of Israel and the Jewish nation. One of the names given to the time of the Apocalypse is, 'the Day of Jacob's Trouble'. Jacob is associated with the Jews and not with the Church of God. This is why Paul wrote that we are 'saved from the coming wrath'. For we have the Blessed Hope of the soon coming of our Lord to gather together His Church and meet us in the air and take us to where He is now. And so shall we ever be with the Lord. So comfort one another with these words because we will play no act or part in the coming Great Tribulation.

CHAPTER 19

# The Sign and Witness of the Great Pyramid

ISAIAH 19:19,20 (NIV), is a very cryptic prophecy pertaining to the Last Days:

> "In that day there will be an alter to the Lord in the heart of Egypt, and a monument to the Lord at its border. It will be a sign and witness to the Lord Almighty in the land of Egypt."

The expression 'that day' is referring to the Day of Wrath or the Day of Tribulation, namely, the Last Days. So this verse is telling us that in the time of the end, there will be some sort of alter or pillar or monument in the heart of Egypt, and on its border, which will be a sign and a witness to God in those days.

In the King James Version, it says this alter will be in the midst or middle of Egypt and on its border. This begs the question, how can an alter or monument be in the middle or heart of a country and on its border at the same time? To crack this riddle we need to know a little of the history of Egypt. In times past, Egypt was divided into two parts; Upper and Lower Egypt. There was a line drawn from east to west which cut across the apex of the Nile

Delta before it splits and drains into the Mediterranean Sea. This line was the border between Upper and Lower Egypt.

Right in the middle of this border, which is in the heart of Egypt, lies a building instantly recognisable as a famous monument or alter or pillar. It is the Great Pyramid of Giza. This is the only monument which fulfils the criteria of being both in the middle of Egypt and on its border at the same time.

But how can the Great Pyramid be a sign and a witness to God Almighty in these, the Last Days? To find the correct answer to this puzzle, we jump forward from the time of Isaiah to the time of Jesus and the Gospel of John and a passage we have already eluded to on a few occasions. But now we look at John 14:2,3 (NIV) for a more lateral perspective:

> "In my Father's house are many rooms...I am going there to prepare a place for you. And if I go and prepare a place for you, I will come back and take you to be with me that you also may be where I am."

We know that after His ascension, Jesus passed through the heavens and now resides in this other location which is in a sort of parallel universe, called heaven. So when people ponder as to whether there is life on other planets in outer space, the answer is an unequivocal, 'Yes'! For the Most High God lives in heaven with His son and the 24 elders and the myriads of good angels. Paul spoke of this heavenly dwelling in 2 Cor 5:1 (NIV):

> "Now we know that if the earthly tent we live in is destroyed, we have a building from God, an eternal house in heaven, not built by human hands."

This eternal house was built by God and it has been receiving an extension for the past 2,000 years as Jesus said he was going there to prepare a place for us. So he has been busy with some building work since his evacuation from this earth after his resurrection. Perhaps he is utilising his carpentry skills in this project?

Hebrews 11:10 (NIV), tells of Abraham and the celestial city he looked forward to:

> "For he was looking forward to the city with foundations whose architect and builder is God."

Speaking of other faithful believers, like Abraham, who lived in the Old Testament, Hebrews 11:15,16 (NIV) has this to say:

> "If they had been thinking of the country they had left, they would have had opportunity to return. Instead they were longing for a better country- a heavenly one.
>
> Therefore God is not ashamed to be called their God, for He has prepared a city for them."

Here it talks of a heavenly country and a city prepared by God. This is obviously referring to heaven and to the place Jesus ascended to. In the next chapter of the same book we are left in no doubt as to this city and its name:

> "But you have come to Mount Zion, to the heavenly Jerusalem, the city of the living God. You have come to thousands upon thousands of angels in joyful assembly, to the church of the firstborn, whose names are written in heaven" Hebrews 12:22,23 (NIV)

And Hebrews 13:14 (NIV) adds:

> "For here we do not have an enduring city, but we are looking for that city that is to come."

All these verses together begin to paint a picture for us of just what heaven is like. It is called a country. There is a city there called Mount Zion. It is the city of the living God and this city is an eternal city and it is yet to come. In this city is the 'Father's house' that Jesus spoke of and it has many rooms. This city and its buildings were not made by human hands but its builder and architect is God. There are thousands upon thousands of joyful spirit men or angels there. There are also a lot of horses in heaven. How do I know that? The Bible tells me so:

> "I saw heaven open and there standing before me was a white horse, whose rider is called Faithful and True. With justice he judges and makes war.
>
> His eyes are like blazing fire and on his head are many crowns. He has a name written on him that no-one knows but he himself.
>
> He is dressed in a robe dipped in blood, and his name is the Word of God. The armies of heaven were following him, riding on white horses and dressed in fine linen, white and clean." Rev19:11-14 (NIV)

As we pointed out already in Rev 17:14, when Jesus returns to defeat the Beast and his armies, with him will be, **'his called, chosen and faithful followers'**. You may have noticed in Heb 12:23 above that it says in heaven along with thousands upon thousands of angels, there is also **'the church of the firstborn'**.

By the time of the final battle at Armageddon, the church or called out of God, who are the firstborn of the spirit of God, are in the Father's house. So when Jesus mounts his white horse to go forth to do battle, we who are faithful and chosen, will be mounting our white steeds to ride at his shoulder.

I have always wanted to be able to ride horses, but a bad hip injury as a teenager prohibited me. Now I am so looking forward to riding horses in heaven in preparation for accompanying the King of kings and Lord of lords when he rides to defeat the forces of evil at the Valley of Megiddo.

The name of this city of God is Mount Zion and the New Jerusalem and this is mentioned by John in Rev 3:12 (NIV):

> "I will write on him the name of my God and the name of the city of my God, the new Jerusalem, which is coming down out of heaven from my God."

After the battle of Armageddon, Jesus is returning to reign on this earth and put this sorry place back together again. He will rule the nations from Jerusalem for 1,000 years. After the battle at Armageddon and the defeat of Satan, the Devil is locked up in the Abyss and Apollo and the False Prophet are cast into the Lake of Fire. This is recorded in Revelation 19:19-21 (NIV):

> "Then I saw the Beast and the kings of the earth and their armies gathered together to make war against the rider on the white horse and his army.
>
> But the Beast was captured and with him the False Prophet who had performed the miraculous signs on his behalf. With these signs he had deluded those who had received the mark of the Beast and worshipped his image.
>
> The two of them were thrown alive in the fiery lake of burning sulphur. The rest of them were killed with the sword that came out of the mouth of the rider on the horse, and all the birds gorged themselves on their flesh."

In the Gospels, Jesus had said that the Lake of Fire was reserved for the Devil and his angels. Because they are spirit, they cannot be destroyed. Therefore they will be eternally in this fiery lake of burning sulphur. Rev 20:1-3 (NIV) continues:

> "And I saw an angel coming down out of heaven having the key to the Abyss and holding in his hand a great chain.
>
> He seized the dragon, that ancient serpent who is the Devil, or Satan, and bound him for a thousand years.
>
> He threw him into the Abyss and locked and sealed it over him, to keep him from deceiving the nations any more until the thousand years were ended. After this, he must be set free for a short time."

(We presume that this angel with the key to the Abyss is the same star that opened the Pit in chapter nine. So perhaps that dilemma is resolved here).

For the duration of the one thousand years that Jesus reigns on this earth, Satan will be locked up in the Abyss where Apollyon and his fallen angels presently are incarcerated. During this thousand years the population of the earth will flourish and grow. This is Paradise Regained with Jesus as King. How blessed a time this will be when we all will be able to see the face of Jesus and live and dine with him. But despite living in a veritable paradise with Jesus as Lord, and to show the utter evil that the heart of man is capable of, there is a rebellion at the conclusion of the millennia.

> "When the thousand years are over, Satan will be released from his prison and will go out to deceive the nations in the four corners of the earth-Gog and Magog-to gather them for battle. In number they are like the sand of the seashore.
>
> They marched across the breadth of the earth and surrounded the camp of God's people, the city He loves.
>
> But fire came down out of heaven and devoured them. And the Devil who deceived them, was thrown into the lake of burning sulphur, where the Beast and the False Prophet had been thrown. They will be tormented day and night forever and ever."
> Rev 20:7-10 (NIV)

I cannot understand that, after everything the world has gone through during the horrific time of the Apocalypse, and having Jesus personally ruling with justice on this earth, that man could rebel and choose to endeavour to destroy all the good that has been achieved. But this is what the Word teaches so we must believe that this is the case. However, the endgame for the Devil and the Antichrist and the False Prophet and the rest of the Nephilim or fallen ones, is that they are all cast into the Lake of Fire, there to reside forever. It is of interest to note that when Satan is thrown into the Lake of Fire after a thousand years, the Antichrist and the False Prophet are still there and have not been destroyed. This is because these are spirit beings and not humans and proves once again, as if we needed more proof, that the Antichrist is indeed a spirit being, an angel who is presently being held in prison in this same Abyss that will be occupied by Satan at the start of the Millennial reign of Christ.

After the crushing of this final rebellion and the demise of Satan, this world will be burned up and there will be established a new heaven and a new earth, wherein dwells righteousness.

> "But the Day of the Lord will come like a thief in the night, in the which the heavens will pass away with a great noise, and the elements shall melt with fervent heat, the earth also and the works that are within shall be burned up.
>
> Looking for and hasting unto the coming of the Day of God, wherein the heavens being on fire shall de dissolved, and the elements shall melt with fervent heat.
>
> Nevertheless we, according to his promise, look for a new heavens and a new earth, wherein dwells righteousness." 2 Peter 3:10,12,13 (KJV)

After the cosmos is burned up and a new heaven and earth are established, John records what he saw in Revelation 21:1,2 (KJV):

> "And I saw a new heaven and a new earth, for the first heaven and first earth were passed away, and there was no more sea.
>
> And I John saw the holy city, New Jerusalem coming down from God out of heaven, prepared as a bride adorned for her husband."

So this city of God, Mount Zion which is presently in heaven, is to come down from heaven and descend to the new earth. Verse 10 on provides a description of this new Jerusalem which will be the capital of the new earth when it arrives:

> "And he carried me away in the spirit to a great and high mountain, and showed me that great city, the holy Jerusalem, descending out of heaven from God.
>
> Having the glory of God; and her light was like unto a stone most precious, even like a jasper stone, clear as crystal.;
>
> And had a wall great and high, and had twelve gates, and at the gates, twelve angels, and names written thereon, which are the names of the twelve tribes of Israel:
>
> And the city lieth four square, and the length is as large as the breadth: and he measured the city with the reed, twelve thousand furlongs. The length and the breadth and the height of it are equal.
>
> And the building of the wall of it was as jasper: and the city was of pure gold, like unto clear glass.
>
> And the foundations of the wall of the city were garnished with all manner of precious stones. The first foundation was jasper; the second, sapphire, the third, chalcedony; the fourth, an emerald.
>
> The fifth, sardonyx; the sixth, sardius; the seventh, chrysolyte; the eight, beryl; the ninth, a topaz; the tenth, a chrysoprasus; the eleventh, a jacinth; the twelfth, an amethyst.
>
> And the twelve gates were twelve pearls; every several gate was of one pearl: and the street of the city was of pure gold, as it were transparent glass." Rev 21:10-21 (KJV)

The interesting thing about this city is that it is made up of elements that are physical and are known and available to us. That is, we know what gold and pearls are. We have sapphires and emerald here on this earth. Yet this holy city, Mount Zion or the New Jerusalem, which now resides in heaven, is made up of these physical stones and other precious elements which are available here on earth. This tells us that presently in heaven, in the Father's house and the city of the living God, are buildings which are constructed with materials which are physical in nature and are well known to us.

This gives us an even fuller idea of what this city in heaven looks like. Plus we know that there must be a lot of horses there ready for Armageddon. So can we presume these horses eat grass and live in fields? There are 24 elders there and thousands of good angels. We saw that when the two angels visited Abraham and Lot, they ate hearty meals. So is there food production going on in heaven to sate the appetites of these spirit men? Why not? We also know that the Devil and the rest of his fallen angels also are in this country for the time being, (it is called a heavenly country in Hebrews 11:15). So perhaps this eternal city and its environs in heaven are not dissimilar to the earth we live in here? Even though heaven is populated by spiritual beings and is in the realm of the spiritual, nevertheless it has physical attributes as evidenced by the materials involved in the city's construction.

Let us examine verse 16 again with regard to the dimensions of this New Jerusalem which is to descend from God out of heaven in the future:

> "The length and the breadth and the height of it are equal."

This brings us back to where we began this chapter and the prophecy in Isaiah 19:19,20. We learned there that the Great Pyramid, which is at the centre of Egypt and on the border, would be a 'sign' and a 'witness' to God Almighty in the Last Days. And when the pyramid in Gaza was originally built, it was finished in a polished white limestone with, according to tradition, a gold capstone to top it off. So what is the Great Pyramid a **'sign of'** and a **'witness to'**?

Well, when we read that the length and the breadth and the height of the New Jerusalem are equal, it becomes obvious that this city of the living God is a pyramid in shape for these are the dimensions of a pyramid. This is why it is called 'Mount' Zion, as 'mount' is the short for mountain. And a mountain puts us in mind of a pyramid. So the Great Pyramid in Egypt is a sign of and a witness to the coming pyramidal city of God which is to descend out of heaven to the new earth in the future. You could say that the Great Pyramid is pointing into the future at the New Jerusalem. And the city of God, Mount Zion, is pointing back at the Great Pyramid. There is a connection between the two. The Great Pyramid in Egypt is an earthly representation of the celestial city of God which is presently in heaven.

Some teach that the new Jerusalem is a cube. But this contradicts the prophecy in Isaiah which intimates that it is pyramidal in shape. For if the New Jerusalem is a cube, then the alter and pillar in the middle of Egypt which is to be a sign of it and a witness to it, would also be a cube!

Also, the length in miles of the height and width of this city is circa 1,400 miles. A cube of that dimension would be a design of poor quality. But a pyramid, on the other hand, is a very symmetric design.

Taking into account all the relevant information provided, I think there is little doubt that the New Jerusalem, Mount Zion which is the city of the living God, is indeed a pyramid in shape. So the alter and pillar which is the monument in the midst of Egypt and on its border, is the Great Pyramid of Giza, and is a sign of and a witness to the coming celestial city of God.

But who built the Great Pyramid originally in Egypt and why was it built at all? And what do the fallen angels have to do with all of this? Well I hope to answer this conundrum now.

CHAPTER 20

# Ancient Monuments and Nephilim Builders

THE GREAT PYRAMID OF Giza in Egypt is the last remaining of the Seven Wonders of the World. It is an astounding monument and a source of wonder for those who have admired it. Originally it was finished in a polished white limestone which would have made it impossible to surmount when it was built some 3,500 years BC. Legend has it that its capstone was covered in gold.

The Great Pyramid stands in almost the exact centre of the world. It is half-way between the northern cape of Norway and the Cape of Good hope in South Africa. It is midway between the west coast of Mexico and the east coast of China and it stands at the intersection of the 30th parallel, both longitude and latitude. It was the tallest structure in the world for almost 5,500 years and is equal to a building 42 storeys high. It contains enough stone to build a six foot high wall from New York to Los Angeles.

The esteemed architect and Biblical scholar, Rev. Clarence Larkin, in his famous book *Dispensational Truths,* came to the following conclusions.

- The base of the Great Pyramid covers about 16 acres. It consists of approximately 2.3 million stone blocks weighing around 2.5 tons each. There are some granite blocks within the pyramid which weigh up to 100 tons each and they are situated at heights of 50 yards up. The sides of this pyramid are equilateral triangles which point exactly to the true north, south, east and west of the earth. The base of the Great Pyramid is a square with the right angles accurate to within one-twentieth of an inch.

- If we take the Hebrew cubit to be 25.025 inches in length, then the length of each side of the base is 365.2422 cubits which is the exact number of days in a solar year including the extra day for every four years. The angle of slope of the sides is 10 to 9. That is, for every ten feet you ascend, you rise in altitude by nine feet. And if you multiply the height of the Great Pyramid by ten raised to the power of nine, you have 91,840,000. This is the exact distance from the earth to the sun in miles.
- The solution to the problem of how to square the circle is embodied in the geometry of the Great Pyramid. Yet what we have been asked to believe by so-called experts, is that ancient Egyptians, or primitive man, wandering in the desert dressed in animal skins thousands of years ago, built this incredible structure. Yet somehow they had not yet invented the wheel!

Of course anyone who has studied the Great Pyramid knows this to be a nonsense. For modern day engineers and architects admit that we, with all our scientific equipment and up-to-date machinery and money, could not replicate the Great Pyramid as it is now. So to believe that ancient man, somewhere between the stone age and the bronze age, built this amazing pyramid, is going from the ridiculous to the sublime.

There are many other mathematical and astronomical anomalies associated with the Great Pyramid which I have detailed in my book on the Nephilim. For instance, there are four 'star shafts' on the north and south face of the pyramid. Each point to four distinct stars; Draco, Sirius, Beta Ursa Minor and Orion. I have identified three of these stars with gods which appear in Greek and Roman and Egyptian mythologies and in the Bible. There are many other pyramids and ancient buildings in several differing parts of the globe that have similar astronomical characteristics. But I won't be delving into these here. Suffice to say that these were all built *not* by half naked savages running around the forests with bones in their noses, but rather by an advanced and sophisticated cabal of beings endowed with superior knowledge and wisdom.

So, back to the Great Pyramid and who built it and why. It is obvious by the above that it was not built by ordinary humans as they did not possess the tools to carry out such a feat. Because it was finished in polished white limestone, you can imagine what an astounding sight it must have been back then, gleaming in the sun of the desert, and it could be seen as far away as the curvature of the earth allowed. So what is the answer as to why it was built, and by whom?

Scholars of the Bible will tell you that Satan always copies or duplicates what the true God does. This is why the Antichrist, when he arrives, will pass himself off as the real Messiah. We pointed out already that he will die and be raised from death by the power of the Devil. This is a counterfeit resurrection (and probably a counterfeit death as well). In 2 Corinthians 11, Paul tells us that it is no marvel that his ministers masquerade as ministers of light, for Satan himself is transformed into an angel of light. Again he is duplicating the true God in so doing.

So when the fallen angels left their first estate, heaven, and manifested on this earth, some 3,200BC, they built this astounding pyramid as a replica of the city of God in heaven, from whence they had come. So the Great Pyramid, in all its original glory, is an earthly duplicate or representation of a celestial reality. It is an image of Mount Zion, the heavenly city of the living God, where abides the divine assembly.

But when Lucifer and his nefarious comrades constructed the Great Pyramid, they did not build it to honour the Most High God. Rather it was built as a monument to their own pride and hubris and arrogance. An earthly symbol of defiance. An icon to insolence.

But how did the Nephilim construct such a monument, I hear you ask? What tools did they employ? The simple answer is that we are not dealing with some inferior species here. These are spirit beings with supernatural knowledge and superhuman strengths. This is evident by some of their doings both in the Old and New Testament times and in the Book of Revelation. For instance, in the time of Moses, when he was vying with Pharaoh to set the children of Israel free, the soothsayers in Pharaoh's court were able to change their staffs into serpents. But Moses changed his wooden staff into a bigger serpent which ate up the others. It takes great power to change an inanimate staff into a living snake.

In the Gospels, when Jesus was tempted of the Devil, Satan was able to levitate Jesus to the pinnacle of the Temple and show him all the glories of the world in a moment of time. This takes great power. And of course in the Book of Revelation, the False Prophet is able to breath life into an image of the Beast and bring it to life and do other miraculous signs and wonders. So for these potent spirit men to construct the Great Pyramid is mere child's play.

There are many other ancient buildings scattered around the world that date back to primitive eras which would have been impossible for primordial man to build. For the natives which populated the areas where these buildings are, possessed very primitive tools and used bows and arrows for hunting and war.

Yet the stone constructs such as at Ankor Wat in Cambodia and the Pyramids in Mexico, to name but two, are of such a high degree of engineering which would make it impossible for natives to do. Indeed, we would be hard-pressed to build replicas of these today, even with modern technology.

No. There can be only one answer. All these ancient structures, many of which have astronomical connections, had to be built by a secret clique of paranormal and mystical spirit men who fell from heaven to earth and had all the mighty power of hell at their disposal. It is these who built the Great Pyramid in the middle of Egypt and on its border, as a mirror of heaven and the city that awaits there.

But God, in His foreknowledge, has turned this on its head and is using it against them. For the prophecy in Isaiah 19:19,20 tells us that this same pyramid portends something that is to happen at the end of days. And this is the coming of the New Jerusalem when the city of God will descend to alight on the new earth, wherein dwells righteousness. So God has taken this replica pyramid, made by Satan and his minions, and is using this as a sign and a witness pointing to His own true and holy city, Mount Zion, the city of the living God, which is to come down out of heaven from God. Eye has not seen, nor ear heard, neither has it entered into the heart of man, the things that God has prepared for those who love Him.

A few years ago, I received an email from a young New Zealand Christian man who had read my book on the fallen angels and what I call, the Pyramid of the Apocalypse, which is the city of God. He told me that he had a vision while asleep one night. In it he looked up in the sky and saw huge pyramids coming down to earth. Someone shouted, "Look, the Nephilim are here". He said that the fallen angels had descended to earth in these pyramids. He assured me that this was no ordinary dream but a vision from God of the future. Another man in Texas contacted me and told me he had several visions of pyramids landing on earth and beings, whom he said were soulless, coming out of them. Then I found another prophetic dream which was posted on the internet. It was several years old and again described fallen angels coming out of pyramid shaped 'craft'. Now I am not saying that this is what is going to occur. But Joel did say that in the Last Days believers would see visions and dream dreams. And Satan does imitate what God does. So if the fallen angels do arrive to earth in such fashion, they can point to those scriptures which speak of a pyramid city coming to earth such as Revelation 21 and Isaiah 19:19,20, and proclaim that they are the fulfillment of this prophesy. Perhaps this is why it talks of the stars of heaven falling to earth like figs falling from a fig tree shaken by a mighty wind.

## Chapter 21

# Three Plagues of Fire, Smoke and Brimstone

The main thrust of this volume is to provide an in-depth study of the Beast and his New World Order government from the perspective of scripture. It is not my role to go into the secular realm to provide information on the New World Order and who is involved there and what they are up to. If the reader wants more data on the NWO, there is a plethora of information available on the Internet. My job is to detail what the Word has to say on these matters rather than provide profane facts regarding their activities.

I would now like to skim through a few other passages in Revelation pertaining to the Beast and his antichrist government in order to round off our study. I will not be commenting on many aspects of the Apocalypse here as I have covered much of this material in my other works. Rather, I will pick a few sections to make some points which I believe are relevant before finishing up.

In an earlier chapter we learned that the serpents, locusts and scorpions were figures of speech referring to evil spirits who will be manifest in the near approaching Apocalypse. Because the Book of Revelation is quite obtuse and is not in sequence, it takes a knowledge of the scope of the book to try to figure out what certain sections mean in order to endeavour to give a proper interpretation of same. With that in mind, we now return to Rev. 9 and the passage immediately after the section we dissected earlier regarding scorpions etc., being fallen angels. For in this next segment I believe the story changes and the metaphors refer to totally different ideas.

> "The horses and riders I saw in my vision looked like this: Their breastplates were fiery red, dark blue and yellow as sulphur. The heads of the horses resembled the heads of lions and out of their mouths came smoke, fire and sulphur.
>
> A third of mankind was killed by the three plagues, of fire, of smoke and the sulphur that came out of their mouths. The power of the horses was in their mouths and in their tails: for their tails were like snakes, having heads with which they inflict injury."
> Rev 9:17-19 (NIV)

I do not think John is now talking about spirits per se, although it is spiritual evil that is in the background pulling the strings for all the wickedness which will prevail at this time. I believe this is a description of warfare and of nuclear strikes. John says that one third of mankind was killed by the three plagues of fire and smoke and brimstone. This has to be three nuclear strikes because only these possess the firepower to kill, in today's terms, two billion people.

The description of tails like snakes and the power being in their heads by which they inflict injury, sounds like firing missiles which trail snake-like smoke as they soar through the air and their war-heads explode when they hit the target. Here is a further description of the same vision in verses 7-10 (NIV):

> "The locusts looked like horses prepared for battle. On their heads they wore something like crowns of gold, and their faces resembled human faces.
>
> Their hair was like women's hair, and their teeth were like lion's teeth. They had breastplates like breastplates of iron, and the sound of their wings were like the thundering of many horses and chariots rushing into battle.
>
> They had tails and stings like scorpions and in their tails they had power to torment people for five months."

Now this definitely sounds like a description of aerial warfare. He calls them 'horses' because they are a mode of transport. The 'crowns of gold' are helmets worn by pilots. The reference to women's hair might be the blades of helicopters as their wings rotate. And missiles look like the shape of lion's teeth. John talks of their wings being like the sound of many horses and chariots rushing into battle, and the breastplates, or body of the jets, were made of iron. This has to be a description, using his primitive vocabulary, to depict modern jet fighters with roaring engines. Again the stings like scorpions are like those from war planes as they are fatal. The allusion to tormenting people for five months could be a reference to germ warfare.

John could only portray the things he saw in terms of his own understanding. He was an old man in his 90's when he received these visions. He could only use his limited vocabulary based on his own experiences to paint a picture of what he saw of this future revelation. Thus the sound of the engines were like the sound of many horses and chariots rushing into battle. And a horizon filled with hundreds of fighter jets and helicopters he says are locusts, for in his understanding only swarming locusts could fill the air in such a way.

At the end of the Tribulation period, all the armies of the world are gathered together in the Valley of Megiddo which is in northern Israel. It speaks of the 'kings of the east' rising and also mentions an amount of 200 million troops (Rev 9:16). This puts us in mind of China who today has a standing army of 100 million but would have no problem making this 200 million as their population is as great as 1.6 billion. We are told that the Euphrates is dried up to make way for the kings of the east. These kill one third of mankind in their march westward. Putting this together with the one third which are killed by the three plagues of fire and smoke and brimstone, this means two thirds, or four billion people, based on the present population, will be wiped out by the end of the Day of Wrath.

> "Then they gathered the kings together to the place that in Hebrew is called Armageddon. The seventh angel poured out his bowl into the air and out of the temple came a loud voice from the throne saying, "It is done!"
>
> Then there came flashes of lightening, rumblings, peals of thunder and a severe earthquake. No earth-quake like it has ever occurred since man has been on earth, so tremendous was the quake.
>
> The great city split into three parts, and the cities of the nations collapsed. God remembered Babylon the Great and gave her the cup filled with the wine of the fury of His wrath." Rev 16:16-19 (NIV)

A huge army from the east, numbering 200 million, arrives at Armageddon. It would appear that by the end of the Apocalypse, all bets are off and the various powers of the world have fallen out and are seeking the advantage. By this time, other factions have appeared and the ten Super-Nation states have broken up and taken sides and are vying for their own positions. The Antichrist sets up camp in Jerusalem and he and his combined forces are pitted against the huge army of 200 million from the east. All nations of the earth are embroiled in this conflagration. Even though the battle lines are set in northern Israel, every other nation is involved and experiences the consequences as we shall now see. For at some point when all these sides are arrayed against one another at Armageddon, someone pushes the red button. John records what he saw and heard: For then there came…

> **"Flashes of lightening…"** Similar to the flashes of lightening we have all witnessed of missiles being fired into the night sky.
>
> **"Rumblings…"** The distant shudder as huge bombs pound the earth which can be heard and felt miles away.
>
> **"Peals of thunder…"** Made by the sound of the firing cannons and missiles and the impact when they explode.
>
> **"And a severe earthquake like no other…so tremendous was the quake…"** The words 'nuclear strike' were not in John's vocabulary. So when he saw the destruction caused by the impact of thousands upon thousands of bombs and missiles hit their targets, he described it as best he could; earthquake. How do we know it was a nuclear strike? Listen to the next phrase:
>
> **"And the cities of the nations collapsed…"** Listening to John's vision of this final battle where he talks of peals of thunder, rumblings and flashes of lightening, then the cities of the nations collapse; this has to be an all-out nuclear attack. For the only thing that can cause all the cities of all the nations to collapse amid fire and smoke at the same time is, a nuclear strike from all sides.

Are we to be concerned by these prophecies? Of course we are. But should we be worried? No. For those of us who are believers and are saints of God, we are saved from this coming Day of Wrath. But those who say we Christians are mad and deluded, they are the ones who must worry and fear for their lives and the lives of their loved ones. For we will be evacuated off this planet before the Antichrist can appear and the Apocalypse begins. But everyone else must remain to go through this time of testing.

In the meantime, those of us to whom these secrets have been delivered, must do what we can to show those in darkness that there is hope and there is a way to escape all those things which are to soon befall this earth and its occupants.

In the last verse of the above passage it says, '**God remembered Babylon the Great and gave her the cup filled with wine of the fury of His wrath'**. This is referring back to that great city which is termed Mystery Babylon and we identified as possibly being New York, which is the headquarters of the Beast and his New World Order and one-world UN government. We suggested that this city would be the target of a nuclear attack. This verse confirms this and also gives us the timing. It will receive the nuclear strike when Armageddon happens and the deadly payload of nuclear weapons from all parts of the earth are fired off and pass each other as they criss-cross the world on their way to the destruction of the cities of the nations. This is why the Beast has as his name, the Destroyer. For by the time the Battle of Armageddon is over, up to four billion of the world's population will be dead.

EPILOGUE

# And the Good News is?

AS WITH MUCH THAT has been written thus far in this volume, we are not asked to understand everything, but we are asked to believe. So much in the Book of Revelation, as elsewhere in scripture, seems so far-fetched as to be stranger than fiction. Yet what is prophesied will happen as it is written. And although many of the miracles performed by Jesus himself are deemed mere fables by those who disbelieve, yet we who are saved know them to be true.

As it was, so shall it be. Beautiful looking gods manifested upon the earth a thousand years or so before the Flood. These powerful and handsome men were irresistible to women who bare giants to them. A similar irruption occurred again after the Flood when a second band of angels descended to earth and had sex with human women. After the departure of the *ekklesia*, these gods will again be manifested on planet earth, much to the astonishment of the world's populace. The proliferation of spiritual and magical films and books in these days, is preparing the way for their appearance.

All the signs of the Apocalypse are happening now and will accelerate and accentuate as the day draws closer. Wars and rumours of wars, increases in famines, diseases and devastating weather patterns will accrue, just as a woman in labour pains. Tensions in the Middle East will increase and continue to occupy the power brokers of world politics. All these point to the soon coming of Jesus to collect his chosen and called. Our days are numbered. For those of us who are saved, all this is good news.

But for those who have not yet received the gospel of salvation and saving grace, the outlook is bleak and about the get much worse.

> "For the testimony of Jesus is the spirit of prophecy."
> Rev 19:10

This is one of my favorite verses in this exciting Book of the Revelation. For I love to spread the Word of Jesus and delight to think of a soul being saved because someone read these words and accepted Jesus as a result. As we cast our bread on the waters, so the Word will not come back void.

If you have been motivated by reading this book, then please pass it on. Many of the people you know who are not yet Christians will be those who will suffer the woeful events prophesied about them in Scripture. If they fail to receive salvation prior to the gathering together of the Church, then this book may act as a legacy to help them through the Tribulation. God bless you and thank you.

208

# ABOUT THE AUTHOR

Patrick Heron was born in Dublin, Ireland in 1952. At age 24 he had a 'Saul on the road to Damascus' type epiphany while reading the Bible. Thus began his Christian walk. Around the mid 90's he got interested in End Times studies. He wanted to make this information available to the ordinary 'man in the street,' and published his first book, *Apocalypse Soon*, in 1997 which became a bestseller in Ireland.

He followed up two years later with *The Apocalypse Generation*. Then in 2004, he published his most successful book, *The Nephilim and the Pyramid of the Apocalypse.* It immediately shot to number one bestseller in the 'prophecy' section of Amazon Books where it remained for almost two years. The Nephilim is widely accepted as being a seminal work on the topic of the fallen angels of Genesis 6 and continues to receive critical acclaim. It has been translated into Korean, Spanish, and Portuguese as in available in Spain, Brazil and Argentina.

Because of the research in this book, Patrick Heron received an honorary Doctorate in Christian Literature from the California Pacific School of Theology. He also holds a B.Sc. and an MA in Business and a B.Sc. in Theology. Grizzly Adams Productions have made two documentary films featuring Patrick Heron and his work which have featured on dozens of TV stations across the USA. The best known of these is, *Apocalypse and the End Times.*

Patrick Heron's latest book, *Return of the Antichrist and the New World Order,* is another seminal and pioneering work and the first in-depth study of the man who is named 33 times in the Book of Revelation as The Beast from the Abyss. This book will challenge widely held beliefs concerning the coming Antichrist and is set to be a controversial and revisionist volume which will explode and debunk many of the accepted facts concerning this individual. His conclusions are taken exclusively from scripture. This book is availible to download on Amazon Kindle and other iBook readers and is also available as an Audio Book (See www.neph.ie).

Patrick Heron has featured on hundreds of radio and TV stations both in the USA and internationally. He has spoken at several international conferences and his DVD, *The Return of the Nephilim*, has been widely viewed. If you would like to translate any of Patrick Herons books into another language, please contact the author. Patrick lives and runs a business in Dublin with his wife Catherine and has three daughters, Emily, Leah and Klara.

If you would like to book Patrick Heron for an interview, he can be contacted through his website: *www.neph.ie*